Meaningful Workplaces

Meaningful Workplaces

Reframing How and Where We Work

NEAL CHALOFSKY

JOSSEY-BASS
A Wiley Imprint
www.josseybass.com

Library of Congress Cataloging-in-Publication Data

Chalofsky, Neal, 1945-
    Meaningful workplaces : reframing how and where we work / Neal Chalofsky.
        p. cm.
    Includes bibliographical references and index.
    ISBN 978-0-470-40300-6
    1. Work environment.   2. Corporate culture.   I. Title.
    HD7261.C427 2010
    658.3'8—dc22

                                                    2010003896

CONTENTS

SECTION ONE

Meaningful Work

SECTION TWO

Meaningful Workplaces

MEANINGFUL WORK is like motherhood and apple pie: who wouldn't want it? In addition, who wouldn't want to do it in a humanistic organization? There are numerous books that will tell you it's all about finding your passion, so why does the marketplace need another one? Well, the reason that it took me several years and a giant mound of resources is that meaningful work is not just about finding your passion. That's part of it, but both individuals and organizations need to realize that there is a lot more that goes into finding meaningful work and developing a values-based organizational culture than just finding your passion or offering your employees a bunch of perks.

Like most issues involving individual motivation and organizational effectiveness, there is no quick fix. So this book doesn't take a ten-steps approach. Good professional career counselors will tell you it takes hard work and dedication to find what you really want to do and then go out and find the actual work or workplace that furnishes the "space" for you to do it. Good professional management consultants will tell you it takes a lot of time and commitment to change, or maintain, a values-based culture. Even with all the evidence suggesting organizations that care about their people perform better than those that don't, many organizations are still not convinced of the value of such a culture, or at best they pay lip service to it.

My Journey and What I Learned from It

My story is about making choices as to the work I wanted to do and how I wanted to do it, and then later realizing the benefits stemming from the choices I made. I went straight into an MBA program after graduating college, and then I took a job working in a small personnel office of a computer systems company that had a contract with NASA's Goddard Space Flight Center. After spending three years screening computer systems specialists, I was asked to design a training program for supervisors on new personnel policies and procedures instituted by corporate HQ. I sought help from one of my MBA professors, designed and conducted the course, and then realized I had found something that interested me far more than reading resumes. So I asked one of our recruiting firms to help me find a job in training. I ended up being employed by a two-person consulting firm that was looking for someone to do administrative and logistical tasks in support of its training programs. I left them after a year and went with a larger firm, where I slowly began to do some training design and instruction.

Ironically, while working on a training program with the consulting firm back at NASA/Goddard, I was noticed by one of the internal training specialists, who suggested I might be interested in a job with NASA. After conferring with my boss, who encouraged me to apply, I started work as a training specialist at Goddard, as a federal employee. It helped that those were the glory days at NASA, when the space program was extremely popular with the public and we in the training department were encouraged to be creative, experiment, and hire just about any outside expert or consulting service we wanted. One of the strategies our director instituted was that we were to work hand in hand with any outside consultant we hired. Our director left NASA when he was asked to head up human resource development (HRD) for all of (what is now) the Department of Health and Human Services. Bringing me along to direct a new executive development program, he instituted the same policy of hiring consultants at the Office of the Secretary, and since I was dealing with the leadership of the department I was able to bring in the nation's top consultants and academics. He also gave me the autonomy to design and equip a new facility for our program that befit the clientele we were serving.

While I was at NASA, I got involved with the local chapter of the American Society for Training and Development (ASTD) and began a doctoral program part-time at the George Washington University in HRD and organization behavior. At ASTD, I joined committees and volunteered for projects that gave me tremendous opportunities for learning and networking with fellow professionals, as well as with some of the top consultants and leaders in the field. My last job in the federal government was my most meaningful. I was looking around for an agency that could be a site for my dissertation and happened upon a unit of the U.S. Office of Personnel Management that conducted research and development projects focused on HRD in the federal government. I spent the next five years working under an extremely enlightened manager who allowed us to work in teams of our own choosing, permitted us to work wherever we wanted (before the days of telecommuting and virtual groups), and even let us hire our own supervisor.

The division I was in was reorganized, and I started to lose interest in my new job responsibilities. I was adjunct teaching at George Washington University and the Virginia Tech Graduate Center when I heard about a full-time faculty position at the Virginia Tech Graduate Center to design and establish a new HRD master's and doctoral program. At the same time, my wife and I decided to start a family, which meant she stopped working when our first child arrived while I started a job that paid about half of what I was making in the federal government.

I discovered that not only can a couple live on less than they are used to, but the freedom, the autonomy, and the resulting work-life balance of academic life was priceless. Looking back, the ability to be a parent helper at a coop nursery school, go on student field trips, work at home when a family member was sick, and do quality care giving for our adopted son while my wife built a new career were experiences I never would have had in a typical nine-to-five job. In addition, I also discovered where I belonged. Academia and I were a perfect fit.

Looking back, I can identify the key factors that helped me pursue a meaningful career.

To paraphrase a comic strip I use in the classroom, "My parents wanted me to make a good living; I wanted to have a good life." My career was never about the money (although I made a good living in the federal government). In fact, when I reached the highest pay grade for a nonsupervisor, I announced to my boss that I wasn't interested in going any higher. Back in NASA, I saw scientists and engineers who hated being in supervisory positions because it took them away from the work they loved.

I was blessed with a series of bosses who really cared about me as an individual and about my development as a professional. We now know how important an individual's relationship with the direct supervisor is. I had the supportive relationships throughout my years in consulting and the federal government that allowed me to move into a more independent environment in academia with self-confidence.

I had (and still have) a spouse who believed, along with me, in a mutually supportive and risk-taking relationship that has allowed both of us to achieve real balance among work, family, friends, and involvement in our community.

I had a professional network of colleagues through work and volunteer activities whom I could trust to give me feedback, share resources, lend a helping hand when needed, and challenge me to question, think critically, reflect, and learn.

Reframing Our Thinking About Work

The subtitle of the book, *reframing how and where we work*, arises from the premise that we need to think differently about the centrality of work in our lives. We must reframe our mind-set from seeing work as a major life activity we have to put up with to seeing it as a major life activity we should make the most of. We need to reframe the workplace from a space where we go to do our work to a space filled with human relationships based on values of caring, supporting, collaborating, and commitment.

This book is for HR managers, chief learning officers, organizational development consultants (internal and external), thoughtful organizational executives and managers, and individuals who want to assist their organization, their subordinate managers, their direct reports, their stakeholders, their friends and family, and themselves to see the win-win that can result from having meaningful work in a meaningful workplace.

I was lucky to have my work life turn out the way it did. What I have learned from the literature and field research I conducted; the numerous colleagues, students, and friends I talked with; and my own self-reflection is that even though I may have fallen into a career path that worked for me, one does not have to rely just on luck. There are tremendous benefits to understanding what goes into finding meaningful work for yourself or creating it for others. The same goes for creating, maintaining, and working in a values-based organizational culture.

If you are going to spend most of your life at work, why not enjoy it?

Neal Chalofsky
November 2009

Why Is This Topic Important?

There are books on the market that relate to meaningful work and workplaces in such subject areas as personal change, career development, motivation, trust, work-life balance, best organizations to work for, and so on. But none of them offer a substantive account of what constitutes meaningful work and a meaningful workplace, so that individuals can be educated as to what goes into finding or creating fulfilling work, and managers and consultants can understand what it takes to create and sustain a meaningful workplace. As with most issues involving individual motivation and organizational effectiveness, there are no quick fixes. So this book doesn't take a step-by-step approach. Good professional career counselors will tell you hard work and dedication are required to find what you really want to do and then find the actual work or workplace that presents the "space" for you to do it. Good professional management consultants will tell you that it takes time and commitment to change or maintain a values-based culture. Even with all the evidence of organizations that care about their people performing better than those that don't, many organizations are still not convinced of the value of such a culture, or at best they pay lip service to it. This book is about what it takes to have a workplace meeting the needs of *all* the stakeholders: employees, management, the community, suppliers, customers, and society as a whole.

What Can You Achieve with This Book?

This book establishes a framework for understanding the components of meaningful work and the criteria for building and sustaining meaningful workplaces. There are examples and descriptions of the various elements and criteria, as well as discussion of various issues confronting meaningful work-places. As a result of reading this book, you will be able to develop a job search, career plan, and work structures for meaningful work for yourself, your employees, and your clients. In addition, you will be able to create or maintain a meaningful workplace that promotes a values-based, community-oriented organizational culture.

How Is This Book Organized?

The first section covers a model for meaningful work that has been developed from previous literature and continuing research. The model comprises three elements, a sense of self, the work itself, and sense of balance. There is a chapter on each element that explains and expands the concepts with examples and related issues. The second section explores meaningful workplaces and their characteristics, such as values-based organizational culture, meaningful leadership, work-life effectiveness, social responsibility, engagement and commitment, and the concept of work community. Examples of actual organizations are discussed throughout this section. The final chapter combines the individual and organizations levels under the concept of integrated wholeness.

Benefits from This Book

Meaningful Workplaces serves a variety of readers, in seeking to:

- Give an understanding of the complex and deeply felt intrinsic need to have meaningful work that is fulfilling

- Help managers, professionals, and consultants appreciate what really motivates employees to do not just good work but excellent work

- Explain the critical role of learning in developing and performing meaningful work

- Emphasize the need for a values-based organizational culture that is in alignment with a supportive leadership style, social responsibility, commitment to work-life effectiveness, and a community-based environment

- Explore the relationship between a values-based culture and the popular concepts of engagement and commitment

- Support the bottom-line business case for meaningful workplaces

I **WOULD LIKE** first to acknowledge the individual managers and my academic advisor who were my role models of servant leaders and mentors: Dave Booker, Hal Neufeld, Chuck McCarty, Chet Wright, and Len Nadler. I would also like to acknowledge two executives who were truly transformational leaders, Richard (Mac) McCullough and Peter Smith. I would like to thank all of my colleagues over the years, my network of fellow professionals through ASTD, the HRD Consortium, and the Academy of HRD, and my thirty years' worth of students for all my learning and growth. I want to thank Paul Butler for the thoughtful review he did of the first half of the book, and for numerous discussions about meaningful work. I also want to acknowledge the support of Rubens Pessanha Filho, who provided me with editorial and psychological support as my graduate assistant. I appreciate the support of the Jossey-Bass staff: Matthew Davis, Lindsay Morton, Kathleen Dolan Davies, and Carolyn Dumore and Tom Finnegan.

Finally, thanks go to my wonderful family, without whom my life journey would be meaningless: our children, Leah, Ari, Rebecca, and Patrick; Leah's husband, Dylan; Rebecca's husband, Shawn; our grandchildren, Elliott, Levey, and Caiden; and my best friend and soulmate of thirty-eight years, my wife, Margie.

Meaningful Workplaces

Reframing the Nature of Work

WHEN YOU ASK people why they work, their first response usually has to do with money—either the salary itself or what it can buy. When you push past the economic issue of needing to make money to live, you hear about wanting to do something worthwhile with their lives. Even if you ask people who have won the lottery or who have inherited a lot of money why they are still working, their answer usually has to do with satisfying a need to do something fulfilling. People feel good about their accomplishments, whether it's how their home or yard looks, how they coached their children's soccer team, or how they fixed the dishwasher without help.

But how many of us really feel good about our paid work? Survey after survey has told us that the majority of working Americans are not happy in their work. Accomplishment at work is often about meeting deadlines or quotas, not about feeling fulfilled. How many of us can identify people we see day to day who seem happy about their work? In Studs Terkel's famous book *Working* (1974), we saw glimpses of people who were proud of their work, whether it was checking food at a supermarket, digging a grave, or waiting on tables. Back in the seventies, people might have worked at the same job or in the same organization for years but still felt good about their competence and their commitment. The 1970s were a slower age; workers had more time to spend on getting their work completed and appreciating it.

Now needing to do more with less means having little time for creativity or independent thought. For some, though, making time for creativity and independent thought is the furthest thing from their mind.

Read Barbara Ehrenreich's *Nickel and Dimed* (2001) or David Shipler's *Working Poor* (1996) and you discover that the same type of blue-collar and service workers I've just described are those who can't make ends meet because of low wages. They can't afford to rent an apartment, so they live in cheap motel rooms, eat only fast food, and forgo time off work to deal with sickness because they are afraid of being fired. Even if they could take time off, they can't afford to pay for medical care because they have no health insurance.

On one end of the work spectrum, we have people so burdened by their work and personal situations that it's a wonder they make it through the day, let alone think about meaningful work. On the other end, we have people who are financially successful but look back and question whether all the sixty-hour (and more) weeks and weekends without family or personal time were worth it. Then there are the sons and daughters of this generation coming out of high school and college after having grown up as latchkey kids of a single working mother or dual-career parents. They are also questioning why their parents spent so much time at work, and vowing that work-life balance is going to be a critical goal of their work lives.

What Is Missing?

According to one consulting group, when you ask people how they feel about work, they talk about a sense of loss; lack of purpose, trust, and commitment; a loosening of emotional ties to the workplace; and questioning whether their work is worthwhile (Holbrecke and Springett, 2004). People believe they can no longer assume their organization will protect their interests; there is now widespread recognition that they have to take care of themselves, continue to learn and develop throughout their lives, and be responsible for managing their own careers. People are feeling less connected at home and at work; they work longer hours and spend what little leisure time they have with family or watching TV. They don't have the time to make community connections. Many people are so busy at work and so tired when they get home that they may not see a neighbor for weeks on end, much less know them more than just to say hello. Consequently, the workplace might be the only community they know. But it is often a dog-eat-dog and morally hollow atmosphere where distrust and competition are the norm.

Our culture has put human development in the service of economic development. Learning, skill development, and mastery of talent are more about increasing one's ability to be productive or make money than about developing one's human potential. We are socialized to make more money in order to buy more. We want to buy more because success is measured by material possessions. We brag about our material possessions, but we have no time to use (much less enjoy) them. We buy SUVs but never use them in the way they were designed (for off-road trips). We buy top-of-the-line outdoor grills but don't have time to cook out. We buy sophisticated surround-sound audio equipment but don't sit down long enough to listen to music. Sadly, we don't even get the satisfaction of feeling good about our career growth in the first place, because it's just the means to an end. At the "end," baby boomers who are the generation now reaching retirement are looking back and wondering whether all the time spent at work was really worthwhile, even if they are financially well off.

What Happened

The village blacksmith shop was abandoned, the roadside shoe shop was deserted, the tailor left his bench, and all together these mechanics [workers] turned away from their country homes and wended their way to the cities wherein the large factories had been erected. The gates were unlocked in the morning to allow them to enter, and after their daily tasks were done the gates were closed after them in the evening. Silently and thoughtfully, these men went to their homes. They no longer carried the keys of the workshop, for the workshop, tools and key belong not to them, but to their master.

—*Terrence Powderly, grand master workman, Knights of Labor,*
United States, 1889, in Briskin (1996, p. 91)

A more contemporary poem by a GM autoworker has a similar theme:
Are these men and women
Workers of the world?
or is it an overgrown nursery
with children—goosing, slappin, boys
giggling, snotty girls?
What is it about that entrance way,
Those gates to the plant? Is it the
guards, showing your badge—the smell?
Is there some invisible eye
That pierces you through and
transforms your being? Some aura
or ether, that brain and spirit washes you
and commands, "For eight hours
you shall be different."
What is it that instantaneously makes
a child out of a man?
Moments before he was a father, a husband,
an owner of property,
a voter, a lover, an adult.
When he spoke at least some listened.
Salesmen courted his favor.
Insurance men appealed to his family responsibility
and by chance the church sought his help. . . .
But that was before he shuffled past the guard,
climbed the steps,
hung his coat up and
took his place along the line

—Anonymous, in Peters and Waterman (1982, p. 235)

When people lived in villages, there was an intimate connection between
the work they did and the community that benefited from their products
and services. They grew vegetables and sold them at the village market, or
they owned the cobbler shop and made everyone's shoes, or they were the

town blacksmith and shod everyone's horses. They socialized with these same people, as well as helping them when they were in need. Work, family, leisure, religion, and community were intertwined.

In 1860, half the working population was self-employed; by 1900, two-thirds were wage earners. The clock, uniform standards, and supervisors governed work. Alan Briskin (1996), author of *The Stirring of Soul in the Workplace,* noted, "Reason demanded that workers subordinate their own experience of natural rhythms to the logic of efficiency." Briskin described how Oliver Evans, who mechanized the process of milling grain in 1790, utterly and irrevocably changed the nature of work. His system of mechanized movement of processing grain along a conveyor system meant that human hands now touched the product only as they fed the raw materials into the system and removed the finished product at the end of the process. "Evans's mechanized milling machine suggested the emerging value of tying work processes to ever increasing production. Individuals could now serve the machine: watching it, tending to its upkeep, tallying its daily production" (p. 96). Evans created the concept of efficiency, more productivity with less labor. The milling machine gave rise to mass production, which also added the aspect of control.

Men no longer worked in a shop next to their house. Now they worked in buildings called factories or offices, and there was little or no contact between the organization where employees worked and the community where they lived. Work was no longer an integral part of community life; it was detached, controlled, and organized within specific buildings and times. The organization structure did not resemble a community; it was based on a command-and-control concept borrowed from the military. Everyone had a specific responsibility and reported to a supervisor, who reported to layers of managers and executives, who finally reported to the owner. Karl Marx criticized capitalism because it alienated workers from their work, since they neither controlled it nor benefited from its economic rewards.

Then owners started to seek investors, called stockholders, to invest their money in their company so they could have enough money to grow the company. The people who invested their money in stocks in essence became absentee owners. Employees received pay for the work they performed, and owner-investors received dividends based on the profits of the company. There usually was no contact between owner-investors and employees. Within the organization, hierarchy separated executives from workers, and internal competition pitted workers against workers as they fought to move up the ever narrower upper levels of the organization. There was little or no contact between executives and workers. In 1990, the average CEO's pay was 41 times the average worker's pay; in 2008 it was approximately 360 times as much (which actually was a drop off from a high of 525 times worker pay, in 2000; Anderson, Cavanaugh, Collins, Pizzigatti, & Lapham, 2008).

Bernard Sievers (1984), a German OD professor, wrote a profound essay hypothesizing that motivation became an issue only because meaning disappeared once work became separated from the rest of life and community: "Motivation only became an issue—for the social sciences as well as for the organization of work itself—when meaning either disappeared or was lost from work; the loss of meaning of work is immediately connected with the increasing amount of differentiation and fragmentation, with the way work has been, and still is organized in the majority of our Western enterprises. As a consequence, motivation theories have become surrogates for the search of meaning" (p. 3). Meaning was always an integral aspect of work when work was an integral aspect of the life of the community. Work essentially became boring and repetitive, the workplace just a building where work was performed, and management were people who ensured the work got accomplished. As a matter of fact, it does not seem to be accidental that the early attempts to restructure work in order to increase motivation were sold originally as "job redesign." This approach expresses and admits that work has been reduced and fragmented in our organizations very well. The notion that work very often seems to be the label for what has been left over after all the meaningful aspects have been taken away and then has to be enriched and flavored artificially.

If motivation is a surrogate for meaning, then accountability can be considered a surrogate for human connection. If you were making shoes for your neighbor, quality was a given because you were making them for someone you knew. Once we detached work from the community, we removed the human connection between the producer of the product and the customer. Accountability for accomplishing a task substituted for pride in a job well done for a customer you knew. Go to a craft fair and watch how a craftsperson is excited when asked about her product. Work is part of the human condition, but we took the human out of the equation.

The Humanistic Movement in the Workplace

In 1851, the English social critic John Ruskin wrote that "in order for people to be happy in their work, these three things must be needed: they must be fit for it, they must not do too much of it, and they must have a sense of success in it." William Toleman called for industrial betterment programs in 1898 and later expanded on his ideas in a book published in 1909 titled *Social Engineering* (Briskin, 1996). His concept included medical care, profit sharing, and reading rooms for employees, among other benefits. Although he was focusing on the self-interest of owners to retain a more efficient workforce, he emphasized that workers were not machines and would be less effective if not supported. Most industrialists at the time rebuffed his ideas because of the prevalence of what would now be called McGregor's Theory X attitudes.

The person who may have been the first humanist of the twentieth century was actually considered antihumanist by most accounts. Frederick Taylor was most well known for his time and motion studies, which have been considered dehumanizing because they gave management strict control over worker performance. Peter Drucker (1974) asserted that "Taylor, among all his contemporaries, truly deserved the title humanist." For instance, he believed in matching the person's abilities to the complexities of the job and encouraged worker suggestions. He also believed in appropriate training for a job and giving people feedback to help them change. He blamed management for worker restriction of output, rather than worker inferiority. According to Marvin Weisbord (1987), "In short, Taylor sought humane and sensible antidotes to the degradation of work which, like smog and pollution, was an early by-product of the industrial revolution."

The group dynamics movement, and t-group or laboratory training in particular, was the first movement to focus on the human in work groups and later in organizations. The National Training Laboratories, and its counterpart in the UK, Tavistock, worked for recognition of individual and group behavior as the critical component of an effective work group and productive organization. Wilfred Bion and Eric Trist from Tavistock had regular contact with Rensis Likert, Chris Argyris, and others in the states, and the journal *Human Relations* was a joint publication of Tavistock and MIT. This movement later transformed into the organization development concept, which has always had the individual at the heart of its values system.

Humanistic psychology, as represented by such classic theorists as Abraham Maslow, Frederick Herzberg, Douglas McGregor, and Clayton Alderfer, was the driving force to bring meaning back into the workplace. Humanistic psychology was known as the "third force" in the discipline of psychology. The first force emerged out of Freudian psychoanalysis and the depth psychologies of Alfred Adler, Erik Erikson, and Carl Jung, among others. This force focused on the unconscious and thought the conscious, subjective human being was just a manifestation of unconscious drives. The second force was based on Pavlov's work, and represented by application of scientific principles to human behavior as conducted both in the United States and in Great Britain in the early 1900s. The third force was a reaction to these first two forces on the part of such luminaries as Carl Rogers and Maslow, who contended in the 1950s that the subjective human being was important. Also, self-actualization, meaning, intrinsic motivation, and potential were deemed more important than controlling or analyzing behavior.

The Quality of Work Life (QWL) movement evolved out of the work of Trist and others at the Tavistock Institute of Human Relations in England. He and Fred Emory developed the sociotechnical model of human behavior, and QWL was the practical result of their model as applied to organizations. It also fit with the concepts and approaches of the humanistic OD folks. QWL was about development of organizational programs that supported the welfare of employees. It covered everything from security and safety to participation and meaningful work, and it involved unions as well as management. QWL coincided with the corporate social responsibility (CSR) movement, which grew out of concerns about the impact businesses had on the environment. Both movements represented quality of life for employees and society in general. The most recent movement has been referred to as spirituality or meaning at work. The emergence of spirituality in modern business has its roots in multiple sources. The slash-and-burn economics of the 1970s and 1980s generated a workforce strongly antagonistic to certain corporate policies that caused prolonged stress leading to employee burnout, increased absenteeism, medical leave, and turnover costs. Two major social-political series of events triggered concern for spirituality and meaning on a societal level. One set of events was the environmental disasters of Chernobyl, chemical pollution at Bhopal, and big oil spills off the coasts of Canada and Europe. These sparked an increase in the collective conscious about corporate social responsibility. The second set of events was the ethics scandals involving Enron, World-Com, and others. There have been a host of books, articles, and other media questioning our misuse of this planet, the role of work in capitalist societies, and our moral, ethical, and spiritual stance on life's meaning and purpose.

When a more recent, prosperous, tight labor market resulted in an effort to retain employees, the subsequent organizational sensitivity to workforce interests revealed a preference among employees to work for socially responsible, ethically driven organizations that allow the "whole self" to be brought to work. This feeling has increased in the wake of recent ethics scandals. Another source is advances in science and health care, which has established the role of an integrated, holistic approach to health (including the healing power of the mind), capable of mitigating the effects of stress and reducing health care expenses. Finally, the baby boomers in the United States have been going through midlife and early retirement, questioning the meaning and purpose of work in their lives. In addition, such multinational companies as Exxon, AT&T, Boeing, Motorola, Levi Strauss, Intel, and Microsoft, as well as the National Institutes of Health and the World Bank, have found value in exploring and implementing themes of spirituality within their operations. It has often been operationalized as "values-based business."

Reframing the Discussion About Work and Values

Reframing is changing your perspective about how you view a certain situation, usually with the intention of seeing it more positively. Instead of organization leaders, HR managers, and management and OD consultants thinking about how to motivate employees, I use Bernard Sievers's thinking to reframe the discussion to focus on what it is about the work employees perform and the organizations they perform it in that would cause them to look forward to coming to work every day. If one's work were meaningful in and of itself, and the organization a place where one felt safe, valued, and treated well, then we would not need to motivate employees to work.

What Is Meaningful Work?

Gayle (1997) reported that the classic motivation theorists and humanistic psychologists clearly supported the notion of individuals having an inherent need for a work life they believe is meaningful. Maslow (1971) wrote that individuals who do not perceive the workplace as meaningful and purposeful will not work up to their professional capacity. The focus here is on those theories concerned with what Maslow called forces acting "within a person."

Maslow (1943, 1954, 1970, 1971), Herzberg, Mausner, & Snyderman (1959), McClelland (1965), Alderfer (1972), McGregor (1960), and Rogers (1959, 1961) theorized that individuals are motivated to take certain actions on the basis of fulfilling needs believed to be inherent in all humans. As human needs move from basic survival to higher-order, they become more intrinsic and reflective in nature. The higher-order needs are translated to values, working toward a higher cause: meaningfulness and life purpose. A few theorists moved beyond the notion of the value of performing a set of tasks as a primary motivator, most notably Maslow (1971). After establishing his *hierarchy of needs,* he began to explore the meaning of work. This exploration was expressed in his description of "being values," referred to as *B values* (truth, transcendence, goodness, uniqueness, aliveness, justice, richness, meaningfulness). Maslow believed that individuals have the potential to reach what he called self-actualization, which is the process of developing one's potential, of expressing oneself to the fullest possible extent in a manner that is personally fulfilling. It is not an end state but an ongoing process of becoming. Near the end of his life, Maslow wrote of people who seemed to transcend self-actualization. He labeled this phenomenon "Theory Z" after McGregor's Theories X and Y (1960). In the state described by Maslow, people are devoted to a task, vocation, or calling that transcends the dichotomies of work and play. Maslow viewed this as a dynamic process of expanding the capabilities of the self to virtually unlimited potential.

The humanistic theorists all reflected on intrinsic motivation and growth (learning) because organizations were focusing on authority and control and had lost sight of these basic needs. There are two reasons this is important. First, in our rush to get to performance (the end goal) we somehow keep neglecting the importance of the *means* to the end. Second, just as the traditional paradigms around such issues as organizational structure, management style, and career development are no longer valid, neither are the traditional paradigms around motivation and learning.

We still apply these mechanistic paradigms. We haven't altered our approaches to these two elements even though how we work and the environment in which we do our work has changed dramatically.

For quite some time we have believed that intrinsic motivation was about satisfying one's values through performance of a task and satisfaction from accomplishing the task (or job). Although the emphasis may have been on the congruence of the task with our beliefs, objectives, and anticipated rewards, motivation was focused on accomplishment of the task. So we reward accomplishment with money and promotions. But studies have indicated that workers promoted to both low and middle management felt that, though self-actualization needs were of great importance to them, there were few opportunities for these needs to be fulfilled in these positions. We may reward people by promoting them into management, where the work does not offer a sense of self-fulfillment, an opportunity for personal growth and development, or a feeling of worthwhile accomplishment. By contrast, meaning has been found to be *more fundamentally* intrinsic than values, suggesting a third and deeper level of satisfaction than extrinsic and intrinsic. This implies that money and promotions cannot offer meaning.

Meaning *in* work, or *meaningful work*, suggests an inclusive state of being. It is the way we express the meaning and purpose of our lives through the activities (work) that take up most of our waking hours. Work is one of the primary ways of furnishing identity and a reason for functioning as a human being.

Before going any further, I want to clarify several distinctions about the words *meaning* and *work*. Meaning *at* work implies a relationship between the person and the organization or the workplace, in terms of commitment, loyalty, and dedication. In a book sponsored by the Society for Industrial and Organizational Psychology on the changing nature of work (Howard, 1995), the closest any of the chapter authors comes to addressing meaning is by discussing empowerment in the workplace. Meaning *of* work implies a sociological and anthropological concern for the role of work in a society; it is discussed in terms of the norms, values, and traditions of work in the day-to-day life of people. Dubin (1976) uses the term *work centrality* as a general belief about the value of working in one's life. The MOW International Research Team (1987) used this definition as the basis for the framework they used to study the meaning of work in society in eight countries.

Csikszentmihalyi (1990), in his attempt to define meaning, readily acknowledged the difficulty of the task by suggesting that any definition of the term would undoubtedly be circular. However, he points to three ways in which the word may be defined: (1) having a purpose or the significance of something, (2) the intentions one holds, and (3) identifying or clarifying the term in context. Similarly, one may attempt to define *work*. Dirkx (1995) subscribed to the theory that work is one of the ways in which a mature adult cares for oneself and others. This was expressed by respondents in the Schaefer and Darling study (1996), who defined work as an opportunity for service to others and not distinct from the rest of life. The term may also be definitive of one's uniqueness and a way of expressing oneself in the world.

The Roffey Park Institute survey of English companies (Holbrecke and Springett, 2004) drew up this list, when they asked what constitutes meaningful work:

- Connecting with others over time
- Sense of personal purpose
- A heightened understanding of what's really important, of what it is to be human
- Desire to give to others and fulfill themselves in the workplace
- Sense of community

- Higher sense of purpose, especially a customer-focused purpose
- Congruence between personal and organizational values
- Wanting to work for ethical organizations
- Feeling involved and treated as adults
- Work-life balance
- Wanting challenging jobs with personal growth
- Wanting to discuss spirituality

A similar survey conducted in the United States by BlessingWhite found that when respondents were asked what factors they would take into account in looking for a new position, these were the top three factors:

1. Interesting work
   - Challenging
   - Stimulates my intellect
   - Expands my skills
2. Meaningful work
   - Satisfies my personal values
   - Contributes to the larger community
3. Work-life balance

What Is a Meaningful Workplace?

The Great Place to Work Institute, originators of the 100 Best Companies to Work for list, defines a great place to work as a place where employees "trust the people they work for, have pride in what they do, and enjoy the people they work with"—and that a great workplace is measured by the quality of the three interconnected relationships existing there:

1. The relationship between employees and management
2. The relationship between employees and their jobs and company
3. The relationship between employees and other employees (2009 Great Place to Work Institute website, www.greatplacetowork.com/great/index.php)

This all sounds like common sense, but as Jeffrey Pfeffer (1998) has pointed out in his book *The Human Equation*, although research, experience, and common sense should have all organizations putting people before profits, the exact opposite is still operating. Organizations will move further away from putting people first the more the economy goes downhill. Many organizations still react to increased competition and economic downturn with antiquated approaches that may, at best, save some money in the short run but ultimately hurt the organization in the long run. Although it was assumed that the economic downturn in 2009 would suppress sustainable and socially responsible work practices, it actually caused consumers and workers to demand more from organizations in terms of their responsibility to society. It would be quite shortsighted for organizations to not care about sustainability, given the data showing there may still be a labor shortage once the economy turns around.

We need to rethink how we can have both effectiveness and sustainability. One answer is by building meaningful workplaces. Meaningful workplaces have values-based organizational cultures that consider employees just as important as customers, if not more so. In fact, they treat all the stakeholders, stockholders, executives, employees, customers, suppliers, the community, and the larger society *with value.* The culture drives the style of leadership; how people work, grow, and live their lives; the relationship between the organization and the world outside the organization; and their identity and image as a place of work.

The Rest of the Book

The first section covers a model for meaningful work that I have developed based on previous literature and research. This model is relevant to HR and OD professionals, managers, and executives, as well as thoughtful individuals who want more of an understanding about what constitutes meaningful work. The second section explores meaningful workplaces— organizations that have values-based cultures and that are known to be employee-friendly, progressive, and concerned with meaningful work.

Meaningful Work

1

The Elements of Meaningful Work

INTRINSIC MOTIVATION and personal and professional growth are two aspects of individual and organizational behavior that are more critical today than when first proposed and advocated by the legendary motivation theorists Maslow, Hersberg, and Aldefer. In our desire to assist workers and organizations to be more productive, we have forgotten our roots as human resource and organization development professionals, as well as managers and leaders. There are two reasons this is important:

1. In our rush to get to performance (the end goal), we keep neglecting the importance of the means to the end.

2. Traditional paradigms around issues such as organizational structure, management style, and employee benefits are no longer valid, and neither are traditional paradigms around motivation and development.

We haven't changed our approaches to these two elements even though the work we do and the environment in which we do the work have changed dramatically. We are trying to survive and prosper in a service-era and knowledge-era economy with a bureaucratic and manufacturing mind-set.

We also keep trying to fix problems using a mechanistic, cause-and-effect mind-set and then cannot understand why individuals and organizations don't change.

> There is a lot of turmoil, confusion, and pain in the business world today. . . . Managers and human resource people attend workshop after workshop [and call in consultant after consultant], embracing each new tool as a way to create the new workplace, only to see their hopes dashed. They say, "If only we could find the right technique. Surely there must be a way of making best management practices stick." Yet, after a short application, it's back to business as usual.
>
> —*Nirenberg (1995), p. 2*

Nirenberg found that, paradoxically, if the conditions were appropriate and the people open to the application of a given tool, *then the tool itself was often not needed.* Conversely, many organizations block introduction of new ideas such that no tool or technique is going to work; then they use the tool or technique as the scapegoat. In the end, the people who suggested the tool or technique in the first place are blamed for it not being the panacea. As one consultant sized up the dilemma, "Organizations don't change. People change. And then people change organizations" (Richard, 1996, p. 3).

One way of helping people change is to assist them in finding, or offering them, meaningful work. This way the intrinsic motivation and development is built in, so we do not have to find a fix for it or throw perks at it. If people have meaningful work, then they want to do good work, they have commitment to the job and the organization, they act professionally (ethically and responsibly), and they feel fulfilled.

Meaning Plus Work

I want to be clear about the words *meaning* and *work* as I use them. For the sake of comparison, meaning *at* work implies a relationship between the person and the organization or the workplace, in terms of commitment, loyalty, and dedication. Richards (1995) says that if there is meaning at work, "[only then] will our work become more joyful [and] our organizations will flourish with commitment, passion, imagination, spirit, and soul" (p. 94). According to Porters and colleagues (1974), commitment involves the willingness of employees to exert higher efforts on behalf of the organization, a strong desire to stay in the organization, and acceptance of the major goals and values of the organization. I deal with meaning at work in the second half of the book. Meaning *of* work implies a sociological and anthropological concern for the role of work in a society, in terms of the norms, values, and traditions of work in the day-to-day life of people. Dubin (1976) uses the term *work centrality* as a general belief about the value in one's life of working. I do not address this aspect of meaning plus work.

Meaning *in* work, or *meaningful work*, suggests an inclusive state of being. It is how we express the meaning and purpose of our lives through the activities (work) that make up most of our waking hours. For some, work is their life, as reflected in the comments of an unemployed forty-five-year-old construction worker captured in Studs Terkel's *Working* (1974): "Right now I can't really describe myself because . . . I'm unemployed. . . . So, you see, I can't say who I am right now . . . I guess a man's something else besides his work, isn't he? But what? I just don't know." The opposite of meaningful work is alienation, which Wilensky (1960) defined as disassociation of self from work and loss of capacity to express oneself in work. For the purpose of this book, I have chosen *meaningful work* as the term to focus on that which gives essence to what we do and brings a sense of fulfillment to our lives.

Values have usually been considered intrinsic motivators to performing a task and deriving satisfaction from accomplishing a task (or job). Although the emphasis may be on the congruence of the task with our beliefs, objectives, and anticipated rewards, motivation focuses on accomplishing the task. The value is based on what is received as a result of the accomplishment. We are motivated intrinsically by what the outcome or accomplishment gets us in terms of feelings (emotions). Meaning, on the other hand, is more deeply intrinsic than values, suggesting three levels of satisfaction; extrinsic, intrinsic, and something even deeper—meaningful work.

The Meaningful Work Model

This deeper level of intrinsic motivation has to do with work that reflects "the expression of our inner being" (Fox, 1994).

The Meaningful Work Model of Figure 1.1 consists of:

- The sense of self
  - Bringing one's whole self (mind, body, emotion, spirit) to the work (and the workplace)
  - Finding one's purpose in life, and how work fits into that purpose
  - Taking care of the self by taking care of others
  - Developing one's potential
  - Having a positive belief system about achieving one's purpose
  - Being in control
  - Favoring meaningful learning

- The work itself
  - Fulfilling one's purpose
  - Mastering one's performance
  - Seeking learning: challenge, creativity, and continuous growth

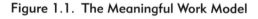

Figure 1.1. The Meaningful Work Model

Copyright ©2003 Neal Chalofsky.

- Pursuing the opportunity to carry out one's purpose through the work
- Having autonomy, empowerment, and a sense of control over one's environment
- The sense of balance
  - Balancing work and the rest of life
  - Balancing career and the rest of life
  - Managing the tensions

No single factor in each of these three elements can stand alone or is more important than the others. Meaningful work requires the interplay of all. We can examine each element separately while acknowledging its interdependence.

Sense of Self

People need to bring their whole selves (mind, body, emotion, and spirit) to their work. The sense of the whole self is critical to finding meaning in work. People often fail to bring their whole selves to work out of fear of rejection, prejudice, or misunderstanding. In his book *Artful Work: Awakening Joy, Meaning, and Commitment in the Workplace,* Richards (1995) said that "we work hard to create physical safety in our workplaces. Can't we also create mental, emotional, and spiritual safety—safety for the whole person?" One of the significant findings of a recent study on spirituality and work was the number of respondents who believed they could not bring their whole self to their present workplace. Before one can bring the whole self to work, one has to first be aware of one's own values, beliefs, and purpose in life. The sense of self also includes constantly striving to reach one's potential, believing in the ability to reach that potential, and realizing the criticality of continuous lifelong learning. The sense of self also includes having control over personal and work "space."

The Work Itself

"Real joy comes not from ease or riches or from the praise of men, but from doing something worthwhile." Wilfred Grenfell's statement (ThinkExist.com, 2008) personifies the essence of what really motivates people. Csikszentmihalyi

(1990) found in his research on high performance that people in what he refers to as a "flow state" actually feel a sense of disappointment when they achieve the objective of their performance, because the act of performing is the motivator, not accomplishment of the task. So the end goal of money or status is not what was of importance; it is the ability to have an impact on the organization's effectiveness through the work, and the self-directed space to be continuously challenged, creative, and learning. In the not-so-distant past, managers made decisions about the structure and process of work activities, in the name of efficiency. Jobs were broken down into tasks, which involved certain competencies as well as specific and measurable objectives. People were hired to perform tightly defined jobs. But work has now changed dramatically. Knowledge workers are hired to bring their skills and abilities to bear on multiple projects having ill-defined goals and boundaries. This requires more worker autonomy, flexibility, empowerment, continuous learning, risk taking, and creativity.

Sense of Balance

To paraphrase a Zen Buddhist saying, work and pleasure should be so aligned that it is impossible to distinguish one from the other. The sense of balance at its ideal is that life is so integrated that it doesn't matter what one is doing, so long as it's meaningful. A sense of balance concerns the choices we make between the time we spend at paid work, unpaid work (work at home, with family, as a volunteer), and pleasurable pursuits. We try to keep up with it all—job, home, community, health, family, and personal relationships—but life doesn't feel fulfilling. We are not doing what we want to do, and we are not acting according to our true values. We feel disconnected from the people who matter most, and we are not taking care of ourselves.

Balance is not a state of being where everything in our lives is apportioned equal weight. Greenhaus, Collins, and Shaw (2003) suggest that balance should be considered from three perspectives:

1. *Time balance* How time is divided between the roles we play at work, at home, with family and friends, in the community, in our religious or spiritual affiliations, etc.

2. *Involvement balance* How our psychological involvement is invested in these roles

3. *Satisfaction balance* How much satisfaction we gain from the roles

Some people say there is no such thing as work-life balance. Work pays the bills and comes first. Balance, though, is not about work opposed to the rest of your life, but about accepting all the parts of your life, in the present and throughout your career, and learning to manage the tensions among (not between) the parts of your life. You do this by looking at how you focus your energy and your time, to make them as enriching and fulfilling as possible. Work-life balance has to do with a sense of balance anchored by a foundation of purpose and meaning, while being flexible enough to bend with changing needs and conditions.

Meaningful work requires the interplay of all of these elements, and they all come together in the term *integrated wholeness* (Maslow, 1943). One of Maslow's earliest works described the key principles to be included in any theory of human motivation. He believed "the integrated wholeness of the organism must be one of the foundation stones of motivation theory" (p. 370). The next three chapters elaborate on the three elements of the Meaningful Work model.

2

Bringing Your Whole Self to Work

I **AM A CARPENTER**," or "I'm a school custodian (or "an accountant," "a therapist," a nanny"), speaks as much to who we are as humans as it does to the collection of tasks we perform for our livelihood. One of the first questions we are asked by strangers after they hear our name is, "What do you do?" But what we *do*, according to Matthew Fox (1994), is the label of the job we get paid for in order to put bread on the table, a roof over our heads, and some extra money for pleasurable pursuits. The work we identify with, on the other hand, is the culmination of years of education, training, practice, and continued improvement of competencies infused with the emotional energy of wanting to do it well and wanting to accomplish something fulfilling and worthwhile. It is the performance of our values, beliefs, moral philosophy, and personality. Work is the very essence of the human condition, one of the major roles we play on the world stage during our lifetime. Just as excellent actors are able to put their whole self into the role they are playing, we ought to be able to put our whole self into our work.

If you are in physical pain, if your daughter is homesick, if you are tormented about your son's drug addiction, if you are worried about your mother's advancing dementia, if you are struggling with your spiritual beliefs around the untimely death of a friend, or if you just don't like your job, then you will not be able to concentrate on the task at hand. You will become disengaged (I discuss the currently popular concept of engagement in a later chapter), you will be unproductive, and you will be unhappy. But if you can bring those parts of your life into the workplace, have them acknowledged as significant concerns, and see them given time and emotional space to be dealt with, then you will be much more able to focus on your work without having them compete for your attention and energy.

Spirituality and Work

Robert Putnam (2000) used a wonderful metaphor, "bowling alone," for a phenomenon he observed in Western society. People are working the equivalent of more than a month more every year than they did a decade ago. Then they sit in their car in traffic for hours going to and from work, and then get home only to have to answer their cell phone or check email. Work is grueling, home life is hectic, and many people experience disconnect from friends, social activities, neighbors, and community life in general. Bowling has always been as much a socializing activity as it is a sport; most people would never think of bowling alone. Mitroff and Denton (1999), in their groundbreaking study of spirituality in the workplace, found that the phrase best describing what people were feeling was a loss of interconnectedness, and what upset them the most was not being able to bring their complete self into the workplace. For those people who felt adrift spiritually, their work and the workplace ceased to be a source of deeper meaning, satisfaction, and connection.

Helping individuals integrate their work and spiritual lives might mean that the hours they spend working in their lifetime are more joyful, balanced and meaningful, and spiritually nourishing (Gibbons, 2007). These more fulfilled individuals might then return to their families, friends, and communities contented, refreshed, and ready to contribute. Because of this integration, one might expect these people to be more ethical and more productive workers—which would benefit their employers. Moreover, a values-based organization culture might help businesses become humane, socially active, and environmentally responsible.

Spiritual beliefs and attitudes are there whether we acknowledge them or not. Even the most secular individual has views on the nature of humanity, on whether the world is essentially safe or hostile, on whether systems are naturally chaotic or ordered, and about how much our own agency or our circumstances determine our future. These beliefs may play out not too subtly, say during a performance appraisal, or while managing a complex project. Understanding employees' work spirit might open the door to a more holistic understanding of human behavior in the workplace that includes spiritual beliefs and practices, and their effects. If organizations were to consider more fully nonmaterial outcomes—that is, their responsibility to employees, society, and the environment—and if individuals were to be more honest, caring, forgiving, humble, other-centered, dedicated, and inspired because of spirituality at work, then organizations and individuals' working lives could be transformed. It seems vital to understand whether or not this might be realistic or achievable in some measure.

Many people equate *spirituality at work* with purpose and meaning. Gibbons defines it as "the search for direction, meaning, inner wholeness, and connectedness to others, to non-human creation and to a transcendent" (p. 11). Beazley (1997) distinguished "sacred spirituality" from "psychological spirituality." He defined psychological spirituality as the faith in a universality of the human spirit that binds all human beings to one another and to the earth, and that instills motivational and sustaining compassion within them for their fellow humans and for the world. This perspective, which Gibbons calls secular spirituality, allows individuals and organizations to see their spiritual self and their organizational culture as holding to values such as caring for and respecting workers' individual needs, the needs of their neighborhood, society, the global community, and the planet. As is discussed later, this perspective is found in organizations that are considered to be great places to work, are socially responsible, and are sustainable.

When Mitroff and Denton asked their respondents what gave them the most meaning and purpose in their job, they prioritized being able to reach their full potential as human beings and association with an ethical organization.

Finding Your Purpose

Maslow's concept of self-actualization (1971) was based on values concerned with working toward a higher cause, meaningfulness, and life purpose. After establishing his *hierarchy of needs,* he explored the meaning of work. He described "being" values, referred to as *B values*: truth, transcendence, goodness, uniqueness, aliveness, justice, richness, and meaningfulness. Values are the foundation of life purpose. Unfortunately, many of us are not consciously aware of our own values. So the act of looking for a job or considering a career is one of making a good living rather than living a good life. Instead we use external criteria such as income potential, status, and image (Imel, 2002).

There are numerous books and articles about how to find your passion (purpose). I believe there are just three aspects you need to be fully aware of: your life values, your strengths, and what you enjoy doing. Of the three, identifying your values may seem to be the most difficult. Actually, there are various instruments that can help you identify all three aspects of purpose. Some of them can be found in the public domain and can be self-interpreted, and some should be interpreted by qualified professionals, such as career counselors. What is important is starting with the question, "Who am I?" rather than "What should I do?" Po Bronson (2002) spent two years listening to nine hundred people share their stories of how they found their purpose. He chose seventy "ordinary" people (not celebrities, or CEOs) to delve deeper into their experiences to get a real sense of how they found themselves, with respect to career.

He discovered that the process was messy. They didn't follow any prescribed steps; they gradually opened to their inner self and listened to what did and didn't feel right. He didn't find any consistent pattern in how people came to listen and act on that inner voice, but he did discover four misconceptions about work and careers.

First, people who found their purpose didn't do it by setting out to make money first and then learn what they really wanted to do with their life after becoming financially comfortable. Actually, he found numerous people who planned on doing just that but got so caught up in making money that they never stopped. Richard Leider, a well-known career counselor, talks about "triggers" that cause people to pause and think about how they are living their life (Webber, 1998a). Divorce, a death in the family, loss of a job, and serious illness all cause people to stop and take stock of their lives. Bronson interviewed one man, an investment banker, who stopped traveling after he came home from a business trip and his two-year-old son didn't recognize him.

People who find their purpose often realize that what it is they really want to do pays less than what they were making, and in many cases it requires some investment of savings or a loan. Yet money doesn't buy happiness and happiness doesn't require that much money. In other words, the happier you are, the less you need. What people must realize is that acquiring material goods, or going to fancy restaurants, or wearing designer clothing doesn't substitute for meaningfulness. Once you are living a meaningful life, you find you don't require those superficial artifacts, so you don't need all the money you were making to buy those things. Fulfilling your purpose is what drives you, not making money. It is amazing how many stories there are in the media of people who left high-paying jobs for much less financially secure but much more purposeful endeavors, and who also discovered how liberated they felt. The rock group the Eagles, in their song "Already Gone," say, "It so often happens that we live our lives in chains, and we don't even know we have the key."

Seth Goldman, president of Honest Tea (President Obama's favorite drink), was always playing with concoctions to quench his thirst after a run or a game of basketball. He was always looking for something with plenty of taste and little or no sugar. One of his Yale Business School professors, Barry Nalebuff, had an interest in the beverage industry and in 1997 was just returning from a trip to India, where he analyzed the tea industry. As they were talking one day, Nalebuff recounted how the bottled tea companies in the United States usually used the lower-quality leftovers from the whole tea leaves. They both remarked how great it would be to come up with an *honest bottled tea* made from high-quality tea leaves. Soon after, Goldman left his job with the Calvert Group, a socially responsible mutual fund, and started playing with tea mixes in his kitchen. The rest, as they say, is history.

Leider suggests answering two simple questions: "What do I want? And how will I know when I get it?" One tool to help begin answering these questions is the Internet. One can browse around to look at websites dedicated to numerous professions and occupations. There are other ways of getting a sense of what you would like to do, such as apprenticing yourself, shadowing someone, or going on informational interviews. Keep a journal, join a group of people who are doing career searches, meditate, and talk to friends and family you trust. Keep asking yourself if a career of interest will allow you to live your values, do something that matters, enjoy the work, and grow as a human being.

Finding Purpose by Helping Others

There is a story about a man who walks up to a field where a large building is being constructed. A number of stonemasons are working, each using a hammer and chisel to carve a piece of stone. The man asks each of the masons the same question: "What are you doing?" "I'm chipping this stone," says the first. "I'm building a wall," says the second. "I'm a skilled tradesman," says another. "I'm supporting my family." "I'm building a church." "I'm worshipping God," says the last mason (Pozzi & Williams, 1997, p. 9). We all have our own level, or perspective, of purpose in relation to ourselves and others. Studs Terkel talked about a bookbinder who loves repairing old books because "a book is a life." For him, purpose is something more than just fixing a book. He is saving something that represents the author's humanness. But it could also be giving to society by saving a valuable artifact for posterity. The waitress who proudly proclaimed, "when I put a plate down, you don't hear a sound," was proud of her skills, as was the mason in the story here who proclaimed he was a skilled tradesman. Purpose for them was about the pride that comes from mastering competencies. But it could also be about being able to contribute to society by delivering the best possible product or service. The gravedigger who constantly honed his skills because "a human body is going into this grave" is also contributing by perceiving the grave as not just a hole in the ground but a resting place that should reflect the value of what is being placed in it.

Turner (2005) found that helping others was critical to the "self-actualizing" people she studied. They saw themselves as people-oriented, as having to connect with those in need and be caring of others. Miller (2008) found in her research on meaningful work across the lifespan that numerous pieces on meaningful work in the literature highlight the importance of social contribution, most speaking to the value of contributing to others as second only to personal fulfillment. As the participants in her study said, "Meaningful work for me means to do something that is going to impact other people's lives and make it better"; "The real meaningful work, you feel good about, is making a difference, helping people, bringing value to them, supporting them, giving good service, giving more than you're asked for"; "Making a positive impact on people; changing their life for the better"; and "Has a positive impact on people's lives, that makes their life better" (p. 66). The Harvard Good Work project defines good work to include "work of expert quality that benefits the broader society" (Gardner, Csikszentmihalyi, & Damon, 2001, p. ix). The Meaning of Work International Research Project (England & Whitely, 1990) found an *obligation* norm; "everyone has a duty to contribute to a society by working" is one of the three major societal components in the meaning of work (p. 69).

I believe the connection among purpose, spirituality, and contribution is that we want *our lives to matter*. Leider believes everyone wants to leave behind some kind of legacy, some kind of personal mark (Webber, 1998a). Fulfillment comes in part from feeling that what we do on this earth makes a difference to other people. In fact, Maslow's views, expressed in *The Farther Reaches* of *Human Nature* (Maslow, 1971), would warrant the term *"selfless-*actualization" rather than self-actualization (Greene & Burke, 2007, p. 119). His last work espoused human development beyond the self in self-actualization. Maslow's message was that people must ultimately move from a focus on self to a focus and concern for other people to achieve the highest level of human nature. People who move beyond self-actualization "are, without a single exception, involved in a cause outside of their skin: in something outside of themselves, some calling or vocation" (Maslow, 1971, p. 42). Meeting the self-actualization needs focuses on achieving a personal identity and complete acceptance of self, and then moving beyond to a higher connection with others.

Self-Actualization and Reaching Your Potential

Maslow defined self-actualization as "the full use and exploitation of talents, capacities, potentialities, etc." (Maslow, 1954, p. 150). Self-actualization is not a static state. It is an ongoing process in which one's capacities are fully, creatively, and joyfully used: "I think of the self-actualizing man not as an ordinary man with something added, but rather as the ordinary man with nothing taken away. The average man is a full human being with dampened and inhibited powers and capacities" (p. 151). We are all born with the potential to reach self-actualization and beyond. Whether we ever achieve our potential depends on a whole host of biological and environmental factors.

Maslow found that all self-actualizing people are dedicated to a vocation or a cause, to growth, and to a commitment to something greater than oneself and success at one's chosen tasks (Project Management Course, 2005). If we think of life as a series of choices, then self-actualization is the process of making every decision a choice for growth. We often have to choose between growth and safety, between progressing and regressing. Each choice has its positive and negative aspects. To choose safety is to remain with the known and the familiar, but to risk becoming stale and bored. To choose growth is to open oneself to new and challenging experiences, but to risk the unknown and possible failure. Growth doesn't happen without risk, and learning doesn't fully happen without some failure.

Self-actualization is a continuous process of developing one's potentialities. It means using one's abilities and intelligence and "working to do well the thing that one wants to do" (Maslow, 1971, p. 48). Great talent or intelligence is not the same as self-actualization; many gifted people fail to use their abilities fully, while others, with perhaps only average abilities, accomplish a great deal. Martin Luther King, Jr., said, "If a man is called to be a street sweeper, he should sweep streets even as Michelangelo painted, or Beethoven composed music, or Shakespeare wrote poetry. He should sweep streets so well that all the hosts of heaven and earth will pause to say, 'Here lived a great street sweeper who did his job well'" (Deger & Gibson, 2007, p. 609).

Self-actualization is about attitude. It is about wanting to do your best and believing you can do your best. It is a never-ending process of continually living, working, and relating to the world rather than to a single accomplishment. We are the key to unshackling the chains of our existence. We make choices based on external data and internal knowledge, experience, and emotions. These choices can and should lead to being proactively involved in our own development. They should also be based on the belief that we can succeed at doing our best, reaching our potential. We are the *primary* agents of our own destiny. Certainly, factors outside of our control can cause barriers to our development, but a positive attitude can go a long way in helping us reach our potential. So self-actualizers start out with the belief that they will reach their potential. Research on people with expert-level sets of competencies bears out the criticality of a positive belief system. Self-actualizers and experts believe they will succeed in what they set out to achieve, so they are motivated by believing that their actions will produce the outcomes they want. This is called self-efficacy (Bandura, 1986). Self-efficacy (self-confidence; belief in self) also influences how much effort people will sustain in an activity, how long they will persevere while confronting barriers, and how resilient they will be in dealing with adverse situations. People with strong self-efficacy see difficult activities as challenges to be overcome rather than tasks to be avoided. They have greater intrinsic motivation and are more deeply focused, and they set the bar higher than do others with less self-efficacy. Because they believe they will succeed, they tend to be calmer and less stressed in their efforts.

Self-Efficacy and Control

Concern is often voiced as to how much control one has over the environment (job, career, life). It is all well and good to want to pursue your purpose and find the right fit in terms of work, but you have to take care of yourself and your family. Bandura (1997) successfully showed that people perceive the world fundamentally differently, according to their level of self-efficacy. People with high self-efficacy are generally of the opinion that they are in control of their own lives, that their own actions and decisions shape their lives. On the other hand, people with low self-efficacy may see their lives as somewhat out of their hands. In addition, possessing a high level of self-efficacy acts to decrease people's potential for experiencing negative stress feelings by increasing their sense of being in control. People feel stressed when they feel out of control because they do not possess the appropriate coping skills and resources to adequately deal with the situation.

So the answer is not that people who are self-actualized or beyond are in control through having power over all aspects of their lives, but instead that they have learned coping mechanisms to deal with the roadblocks and dilemmas they encounter along the way, and they believe they will successfully get past the roadblocks. Learning enables them to obtain the knowledge, experience, understanding, and wisdom to navigate the journey.

Meaningful Learning

The human function that is most critical to reaching your purpose and potential is learning. As you will see in the next chapter, it is also vital to achieving a sense of personal mastery. In fact, it is probably the most critical aspect of achieving truly meaningful work. But there are at least two forces that seem to block people from learning and growing.

Peter Vaill, a professor of management at Antioch University, coined the term *continuous white water* as a metaphor for change. As a participant in one of Vaill's workshops put it, "You never get out of the rapids! No sooner do you begin to digest one change than another one comes along to keep things unstuck. . . . The feeling is one of continuous upset and chaos" (Vaill, 1989, p. 2). Change has changed. The rate and severity of change has increased dramatically. Thus life as a slow ride in a rowboat with the occasional need to steer around a stump in the water or deal with the wake of a motorboat has become a continuous ride down white water rapids. The feeling is one of clinging to a raft as you are being tossed around and not having the ability to get in control of the ride.

The other barrier blocking learning is represented by the phrase "no pain, no gain." M. Scott Peck (1978), author of *The Road Less Traveled*, presented the thesis that what makes life difficult is that the process of confronting problems is a painful one. Many people are either unwilling or unable to suffer this pain, so they cling to their old patterns of thinking and behaving. When they hold on, they fail to work through any crisis; they fail to learn and grow. Letting go of control and confronting the unknown is a terribly difficult thing to do. Consequently they never experience the sense of rejuvenation that accompanies the successful growth experience.

The worldview and value system that has governed learning in North American and European societies for the past three hundred years was formulated in the sixteenth and seventeenth centuries. The metaphor was the world as a machine, which was brought about by revolutionary changes in physics and astronomy. This mechanistic science was based on a new method of inquiry, which involved mathematical description of nature and the analytic method of reasoning. The physical and social sciences of the twentieth century evolved under this paradigm, to dominate not only learning but also work and every other aspect of our society. In this mechanical era, we believed we knew (or could determine) the outcome for every course of action.

Life has been governed by a "cause-and-effect" mentality. If there is a problem, you find out what is causing it, and you fix it. Back in the 1970s, Argyris and Schön (1974) developed the concepts of single-loop and double-loop learning. *Single-loop learning* is when a problem is encountered and solved in a way that permits an individual to function at a basic level. It is like a thermostat that is programmed to know when it is too hot or too cold and turns the heat on or off. By following predetermined rules of operation, the thermostat performs this task because it receives information (the temperature of the room) and takes corrective action. If I push the handle on the toilet and it doesn't flush, I look to see if the handle is broken, or the chain from the flapper came off, or the flapper is defective. It's usually one of those three things. Every problem is easy to fix; no thinking is involved.

But if my son sneaked out of the house last night to help a friend in need, do I punish him for leaving the house without permission, or praise him for helping a friend? Then what if I find out that he brought the friend back to our house because the friend insisted his mother, who is a friend of mine, was abusing him? *Double-loop learning* occurs when a problem is encountered and solved in ways that involve modification of an individual's or organization's underlying norms, values, beliefs, policies, or objectives. The problem and potential solutions don't fit any predetermined rules, or they seem to conflict with an individual's present mind-set. Most of us will choose single-loop learning over double-loop because it's easier to just follow predetermined responses to problems, even if they don't work. That is what Peck was referring to; it is hard to let go of old patterns and try new approaches that challenge our traditional ways of reacting to problems.

What has happened is that even though we now work in a knowledge economy, we still treat learning with a manufacturing, assembly-line mentality. We are trying to navigate the continuous white waters with an industrial era mind-set. We still learn within a single-loop framework (teach me the right answer, or train me, to solve the problem or fix the defect). In the manufacturing era, we believed we knew (or could determine) the outcome for every course of action. In the knowledge era, we are discovering that there are no causal linkages but "rather that in complex systems, possibilities can be known but precise outcomes cannot be predicted" (Nicoll, 1984, p. 10). This means not only that there are multiple ways of knowing, of viewing reality, but also that we will never know all there is to know. We have to accept divergence, multiple perspectives, and incomplete truths. In giving up the search for the one right way, we must give up the notion that reality is based on fact. Reality is socially constructed. Knowing, then, requires engagement and acceptance that it is an interpretive, dynamic act. To learn, we must be continuously open to all possibilities; the Zen phrase "a beginner's mind" captures the essence of this.

The primary paradigm that still underlies learning in our society is what I call the *outcome paradigm* (Chalofsky, 1996). Learning is based on:

- Minimal competence, learning enough to get the work done
- Fear of failure
- Individual performance
- Internal (organizational) competition
- Appraisal and criticism

- The one right answer
- Rational, logical reasoning only
- Outcome only (the goal, the accomplishment)

The outcome paradigm is based on the premise that cause-and-effect thinking produces an outcome mentality ("I need to know just enough to fix the problem, or complete the task, or get the next promotion"). Self-actualizers riding the white water rapids of the knowledge era need to be able to multitask in complex situations that can have numerous and complicated options. Russell Ackoff (1981), a systems theorist, has talked about a spectrum of learning:

data → information → knowledge → understanding → wisdom

He contends that we spend most of our time and effort dealing with the data-to-information end of the spectrum, such that we never get to understanding, and ultimately wisdom. We are becoming so overwhelmed by data and information, and we have so many choices among alternative actions, that we end up having no time and energy to analyze and reflect so as to move to understanding and wisdom.

We need a new paradigm for learning that reflects another way of knowing, a more holistic approach that emphasizes learning as a process rather than just finding the right answer—one that moves:

- From learning based on minimal competence to learning based on continual improvement
- From learning based on fear of failure to learning based on risk taking
- From learning based on individual performance to learning based on team and collective performance
- From learning based on competition to learning based on cooperation and collaboration
- From learning based on appraisal and criticism to learning based on coaching, support, and feedback

- From formal learning to informal learning
- From learning based only on rational, logical reasoning to learning based on whole-brain thinking
- From learning based on one right answer to learning based on multiple answers
- From learning based on outcomes (the destination) to learning based on process (the journey)

Increasing Capacity to Learn

We must increase our ability to take in more information, translate more information into knowledge, increase our processing of knowledge into understanding, and achieve higher wisdom as we move to self-actualization and beyond. Jean Houston, author of *The Possible Human*, talks about the desire to increase capacity for learning by equating most of humankind's present capacity to living in the attic of a house and never visiting the other floors. She, among others, believes we use only about 25 percent of our capacity, at most. She was one of the first educator psychologists to do work on the mind-body connection and its role in increasing learning. The late 1980s and early 1990s were a time of interest in accelerated learning, mind mapping, reflection, and creativity in general. Professionals in the adult learning and human resource development fields understand there are numerous ways of learning and knowing. Left-brain-dominant people tend to process information differently from right-brain-dominant people, and an individual may favor taking in information orally, visually, or kinesthetically. We realize that people have diverse strengths when it comes to learning knowledge and skills. The popular books *Women's Ways of Knowing* and *Women Are from Venus, Men Are from Mars* have given us insight to how women perceive and process information differently from men. National culture plays a significant role in learning, as well as how we were parented and our educational experiences. To take all these genetic and environmental factors in account, we should recognize ways to increase our capacity to take in, analyze, reflect on, and make sense of all we need to know. Let us examine some approaches to increasing learning capacity and becoming a meaningful learner.

Childlike Curiosity

In *Spirited Leading and Learning* (1998), Vaill says being immersed in a learning process is to be continually confronted with "newness." This is about being open not only to new ideas, concepts, perceptions, and so on but also to new interpretations of one's values, beliefs, and understandings. Having a childlike curiosity is about totally open awareness of what is going on around you and insatiable curiosity for knowing and understanding.

We are socialized to think in terms of closure, ending, accomplishment. So we learn in terms of finishing or reaching the goal. We will even shortcut the learning process to be more efficient. Instead, meaningful learners constantly do double-loop learning, reflecting on what is learned in contrast to what is known. In adult learning theory, this is called *transformational learning*—purposefully seeking out experiences that engage and challenge you to question and reflect on how new learning fits with your values, beliefs, and understandings. One consultant I read about in our local newspaper takes executives to playgrounds and has them study the kids at play. Then he has them get down to their level and play with them, climbing the jungle gym, digging in the sandbox, swinging on the swings. In one course, I have my doctoral students who are studying humanistic psychology and learning read a debate between Carl Rogers, the well-known humanistic therapist, and B. F. Skinner, the father of behavioral psychology. They take radically different positions on the subject. Childlike curiosity also has to do with stopping to smell the roses, to be more aware of the present (see the discussion on timeshifting in Chapter Four).

Open to Differences

Purposefully considering different perspectives—"walking in another person's shoes"—means honestly trying to listen and appreciate differences of all kinds. Experiences that immerse you in another perspective are wonderful ways to understand differences. Working or living in another country, working with a type of organization you have never worked with before, or taking a job in a totally new field all help you gain a sense of the larger world. Seek out books and articles that argue unfamiliar sides of an issue. Value the learning that comes from and through human relationships. Work friendships, networking, and communities of practice multiply the chances for encountering divergent thinking and knowing. You can purposefully put yourself in situations that involve interaction with people having perspectives different from yours. Action learning is a technique that puts you in a group with people from other perspectives (sales, human resources, production), to learn about and wrestle with a common problem. You can seek feedback from friends and colleagues who you know will constructively challenge you. Start or join a professional support group, become active in a professional association, take on community-based volunteer experiences, or volunteer for cross-functional and ad hoc task forces.

Awareness of the Total Self

We all know that proper nutrition, exercise, and sleep help us remain sharp, cognitively and emotionally. Movement and exercise can enhance optimal learning. Mental exercise strengthens and renews neural connections in the brain. Meditation, yoga, and tai chi, among other activities, allow the conscious to draw from the unconscious (to make tacit learning explicit).

True wine connoisseurs don't just *drink* wine; they use all five senses to taste wine. They listen to the cork being removed from the bottle, smell the fragrance, observe the color, and feel and taste the acidity and fruitiness on their tongue. Each of our senses, when activated, is taking in information. The more open we are to our surroundings, the more data we take in.

Be aware of what time of the day you tend to be more or less productive. When your body rhythms take a dip, take a walk. Some organizations even furnish space and support for "power naps," massage, or ping-pong and other games. Be aware of how your emotions can turn you off, and what helps to turn you on again (talking to a friend, listening to music). Another thing we know is that the more you are in touch with your values, beliefs, and feelings the more open you are to receiving feedback. Carl Rogers's concept of the *authentic self* means we are also more open to understanding and being comfortable with ourselves, as well as being more understanding and accepting of others. Being aware and comfortable with yourself psychologically is akin to being fit physically. Meaningful learners bring their total self (physical, psychological, spiritual, mental, and moral) to the learning experience.

Open to Possibilities

Creativity is a heavily researched area that has been connected with increasing capacity for learning. Creativity workshops always start with some kind of "thinking out of the box" activity to open participants up to divergent thinking. Being creative allows us to think of possibilities that we would usually never let ourselves consider. Learning creatively allows us to take in information and knowledge we would normally discard or ignore. One approach is to embrace ambiguity, uncertainty, and paradox—what is known as creative tension. Look for beauty in ugliness, ask why bad things happen to good people, try to understand how people can give money away in one situation and count pennies in another. You can go through exercises that simulate creative tension to expand your awareness. Brainstorm how, say, an orange is like a computer. Physically, change the space where you normally sit to think, or try another environment altogether. Runners warm up before running; learners can warm up before learning, by exercising the right brain.

All these elements are interrelated, overlap, and contribute to increasing a person's ability to take in, process, reflect on, and make meaning of information. Our mental models are being hardwired into our brain as early as age five. This means all the learning we encounter is filtered by our mental models from five onward. The more filters we add, or the fewer we eliminate, the less new information is getting through to be processed. In fact, 80 percent of what winds up in the brain for processing is based on what is *already in* the brain, in terms of ideas and feelings. Only 20 percent of what ultimately gets processed by the brain is totally new data. In other words, you see a plastic bottle with clear liquid and your filters say it must be a bottle of water, even if it's an oddly shaped or colored bottle. So already you are examining something with a bias toward what you believe it is. A person with childlike curiosity might first say, "I wonder what that funny-shaped container is," approaching the same bottle with an openness that allows all kinds of options and alternatives.

There is more to be gained from meaningful learning than just increasing learning capacity. *Meaningful learning is intrinsically motivating.* Approaching learning as an act of discovery rather than another work-related task makes the experience more exciting, fun, and fulfilling. A number of studies look at workers who have a performance orientation toward work compared to a learning orientation. A performance orientation is where workers see the goal as accomplishing a task according to a stated criterion of success. A learning orientation involves seeing the same goal as a challenge that sparks a desire to learn and try new ways to do better than the stated criteria of success. Research results consistently demonstrate that workers with the learning orientation achieve higher productivity, and find more enjoyment and satisfaction.

Another benefit is that you are more in control of the learning experience. You are not a passive participant just taking in information; you are actively engaging with the learning; you are involved mentally, emotionally, morally, and physically (if called for). The most meaningful learning experiences are often informal, experiential ones. If you actively commit to a mentoring program, or "shadowing" an executive, or taking on the leadership of a new team, you are going to have more ownership of the learning experience than just sitting in a classroom. If you have ownership of the learning, than you have more of a stake in following through to see that the learning has an impact on your behavior and attitudes. There is more of a commitment to ensure that the learning will use double-loop processing.

Meaningful learners, while stopping to smell the roses, are also continuously scanning the future, looking for new opportunities to learn and grow. Others turn to them for new technologies, new models, new perspectives. They are seen as the people in the know. They are in the know because they want to know, understand, and constantly reshape the mental models they use to view the world. They are the self-directed learners I will be discussing in Chapter Three, for whom learning is imbedded as a natural aspect of whatever kind of work they are doing.

Conclusion

Striving to be all we can be, and bringing all of who we are to the workplace, allows us to be truly authentic. "To thine own self be true," Shakespeare wrote, with relevance to being authentic in work, career, and life. Your work and your career should be aligned with your core self—your values, beliefs, morals, competencies (strengths), and interests.

Carlos Mencia, the creator of Comedy Central's "Mind of Mencia," was one of eighteen brothers and sisters raised by his aunt and uncle in East Los Angeles. He graduated from high school doing well in math and loving electronics, and he enrolled in Cal State Los Angeles in engineering. He also got a job at an insurance company to pay for college, where he started to play the office comedian. Everyone there encouraged him to go into comedy, and so he went to an amateur open-mike night at a local comedy club. "The set maybe lasted for three minutes, but I had actually made up a joke. I stepped offstage and at that moment I knew that this is what I was supposed to do." He dropped out of college and left the insurance company. Comedy helped him discover that his life was *his* life: "I know we live in a capitalist society and I understand that we all want to feel comfortable and secure. But, honestly, I know poor people who are happier than rich people. Nothing can replace happiness and that means finding that peaceful place inside you, whatever that is. Even if it's being a clown instead of an engineer" (Mencia, 2008, p. 60).

3

The Meaning Is in the Work Itself

To Be of Use

The people I love the best
jump into work headfirst
without dallying in the hallows
and swim off with sure strokes almost out of sight.
They seem to become natives of that element,
the black sleek heads of seals
bouncing like half-submerged balls.
I love people who harness themselves,
an ox to a heavy cart,
who pull like water buffalo with massive patience,
who strain in the mud and the muck
to move things forward,
to do what has been done, again and again.
I want to be with people who submerge
in the task, who go into the fields to harvest

and work in a row and pass the bags along,

who are not parlor generals and field deserters

but move in a common rhythm

when the food must come in or the fire be put out.

The work of the world is common as mud.

Botched, it smears the hands, crumbles to dust.

But the thing worth doing well done

has a shape that satisfies, clean and evident.

Greek amphoras for wine or oil,

Hopi vases that hold corn, are put in museums,

but you know they were made to be used.

The pitcher cries for water to carry

And a person for work that is real.

—*Marge Piercy, from* Circles on the Water, *1982*

THERE IS NOTHING like the feeling of a job well done, especially if the work is meaningful. Whether it is completing a project on time and within budget, or crafting a cabinet with all the joints fitting perfectly, or helping a client deal with a complex problem, or even assembling your daughter's new bicycle—a job worth doing is worth doing well.

Extrinsic and Intrinsic Motivation

In the Introduction, I discussed Bernard Sievers's assertion that motivation as a concept and a practice came about because we removed meaning from work when we removed work from being an intrinsic part of the community. The first rewards (and punishments) were based on compliance with the bureaucratic rules and policies that governed primarily manufacturing organizations. *Extrinsic* motivators are external reinforcers that are either instinctual or learned; they are usually deliberately planned and contrived by others for their predicted influence or the natural consequences of the individual's behavior (Axelrod, 2000). Pay certainly is the most common extrinsic motivator, but the list runs the spectrum from stock options and bonuses to an office with a window to perks such as a corporate gym and concierge services. Obviously, the threat of being fired, demoted, losing the office with the window, and being moved to a cubicle are all negative reinforcers. Extrinsic motivators work only if we care about or value the rewards or fear the punishment. If you are up for a promotion on the basis of a good performance appraisal, and you don't care if you are promoted or don't want to be promoted, then getting a promotion ceases to be a motivator. In addition, if you want the promotion because you are unhappy with your job, and you get the promotion but find you are still unhappy with the work, the raise in pay and stature as a motivator will last only a short while.

Frederick Herzberg (Herzberg, Mausner, & Snyderman, 1959), the famous motivation theorist, identified two separate sets of factors that appeared to operate independently to produce job satisfaction and dissatisfaction:

> *Motivators*, or *satisfiers*, are intrinsic to the job and its content. They include elements such as the work itself (which must be meaningful and challenging), responsibility, achievement, recognition, and opportunities for growth and advancement. They motivate people to high performance.

> *Hygiene* or *maintenance factors*, more recently labeled *dissatisfiers*, are elements of the organizational environment or context. They include company policy and administration; salary and fringe benefits; quality of supervision; interpersonal relationships with supervisor, peers, and subordinates; status; job security; and working conditions. The satisfaction of these needs is a foundation for the application of motivators, and the absence of any one of these factors can demotivate.

We all know people who work in less-than-comfortable and supportive working conditions but love their work and don't seem to care about their work environment or infrastructure. We also know people who have a comfortable salary and plenty of organizational perks and still seem unhappy about their work. Herzberg's prescription for improving performance is encapsulated in his often-quoted statement, "If you want people motivated to do a good job, give them a good job to do."

When Herzberg formulated his theory, the world of work was dominated by the manufacturing sector and the predominant organization structure was the bureaucracy. Managers made decisions about the structure and process of work activities in the name of efficiency (Thomas, 2000). Jobs were broken down into tasks, which involved certain competencies and specific and measurable objectives. Today's workplace is more complex, with more judgment-based jobs than production-based ones, and organization structures with more self-management and team-based opportunities. In addition, today's employees are more sophisticated and knowledgeable and much more aware of issues such as fairness, equality, discrimination, and ethical responsibility. "A fair day's work for a fair day's pay" doesn't cut it anymore. So intrinsically motivated workers are far more valuable to an organization and have much more satisfying jobs than extrinsically motivated employees do. Intrinsic motivation has to do with being able to fulfill your purpose, pride in using your strengths to do a good piece of work, control over how you accomplish your tasks, and satisfaction from completing a task (Thomas, 2000). But having meaningful work goes deeper. Csikszentmihalyi (1990) found in his research on high performance that people in what he refers to as a *flow state* actually feel a sense of disappointment when they accomplish their task, because the act of performing is the motivator, not the completion. People in the flow state derive meaning from their work because they believe and know they will succeed and they accept "failure" because it is worth the risk. So success is secondary to the work itself, and risk (and possibly failure) increases the challenge and learning. He found that those in the flow state seem to want to continue working forever and learn additional skills so they can take on more demanding challenges. The thrill is in the journey, not the reaching of the destination. In addition, he found that, as we discussed in an earlier chapter, people who are in the flow state have a sense of control over their work because they feel positive about their ability to handle the challenge. The motivation, the meaning, is in the work itself.

Fulfilling Your Purpose

We have discussed how to find your purpose, but once you identify it you need to turn your purpose into a job that allows you to do the work you were meant to do. One interesting way to explore opportunities is Vocation

Vacation (www.vocationvacation.com), where you can "try on" different jobs. According to their website,

> VocationVacations is the only company that lets people test-drive their dream jobs. We match you up with an expert mentor in the field of your dreams for a one to three day total immersion mentorship. On your dream job "Vocation" you will:

- Work one-on-one with a personal mentor
- Learn the ins and outs of your dream career
- Try on your dream job lifestyle
- Make valuable contacts in your field; and
- Begin plotting a concrete strategy for moving from the job you have to the job you love.

A *Business Week* article (April 26, 2006) described one individual who was an international banker with HSBC. He had done stints in Bahrain, China, Taiwan, Hong Kong, Turkey, and London over the course of seventeen years. "Exciting as a two-decade spin around the globe once was," Ryan says, his chosen profession was simply "not as exciting as it had been." He entered into what he calls "a pretty long period of reflection" regarding his career path and future. Like many suffering from job ennui, he was ready to do something new; the question was how to do it. Having nursed a lifelong love of dogs, Ryan realized he was interested in potentially moving in that direction but was unsure how exactly he could turn his passion into a sustainable career. He signed up to do a two-and-a-half-day VocationVacation working with a doggie day care provider in Massachusetts. The following month, he spent three days working with a dog trainer in Oregon. Fairly quickly, Ryan figured out that he preferred training to day care and was confident he could start his own business in the field. Moreover, he says the experience helped him realize he didn't have to abandon the skills he developed as a banker. Rather, he says, "It became obvious to me that there were a lot of kennels and trainers that were very good with animals, but business was not their specialty." Ryan resigned from HSBC and enrolled in a dog-training school in Missouri for five months to get certified. In January, he launched Beyond Dog Training in Rye, New Hampshire. "It really sounds weird," he says. "But that two-to-three-day experience has really been a linchpin."

Another website for those seeking part-time jobs is www.MyPartTimePRO .com. Their site describes the service as "connect[ing] educated and accomplished professionals with meaningful, legitimate, part-time employment opportunities. The site exclusively communicates positions to educated career veterans who are not seeking traditional, full-time employment . . . Baby Boomers who don't want to, or can't afford to, stop working altogether, Gen Xers who are willing to give up a little income to spend more time with their families (or) Gen Ys who are interested in pursuing multiple part-time positions that reflect both career and personal interests."

Leider recommends that job searching should be considered an adventure. I once had a career consultant tell me that finding a great job was not about luck, but awareness. People tend to limit the scope of their potential opportunities by thinking about jobs as defined only by want ads. One reason people tend to use job ads of various kinds is that it's easier to look in the newspaper or on the Internet than it is to treat the process as an adventure. Also, most people haven't done the front end I described in the last chapter about finding out what you want to do (your purpose) before you go looking for a new job. Note in the earlier story that Ryan did "a pretty long period of reflection" before he realized what he really wanted to pursue. So people usually look for the same job they want to leave or a similar one, even if they are unhappy with the actual work they do. They believe that maybe the same work will be better in another organization. For some this may be the case, but I believe most people realize once they settle in to the new environment that they still are unhappy with the work. Treating the job search as an adventure means exploring, not just sticking a push pin into the first job ad that sounds promising. In fact, many of us in the baby boom generation are still in careers stemming from the first job we got out of school, and that job was based on what was available and seemed to fit what we *thought* we wanted to do or what we were supposedly *educated* to do. Many of us never looked back, so long as we were making enough money to meet our needs or else believed we couldn't do any better.

Another consideration is the environment you want to be in. Leider talks about being clear about what kind of environment best fits your style, temperament, and values. Do you want to work for yourself, be part of a team, be a leader, work nine to five, work in a big organization, have variable hours, work for a small business, work at home, travel to other countries, be in meetings most of the day, not have to commute far to get to and from work, be on the road a lot, have a nice office? Again, most people haven't fully thought out all the variables involved in *where* one wants to work. Later on, starting in Chapter Five we will spell out in more detail what a meaningful workplace looks like; suffice it to say for now that the environment should be one that treats you like a professional. I do not mean professional in the white-collar sense. I mean that you approach your work in a professional manner, no matter what the work is—and your organization regards you as a professional, no matter what the work is. You can work for an organization that either supports you or leaves you alone, or some combination of the two. Leaving you alone means laying out what the job expectations are and then staying out of your way as much as possible to let you determine how best to get it done. It also means still offering support for your continued high performance and development.

Personal Mastery

Susan Gayle (1997) discovered that "gold collar" workers (the top 1 percent of high-technology systems experts) were continuously honing their skills and learning new advances when they were not deeply immersed in their work. They were either improving themselves or improving the systems they were working on. So the end goal of money or status was not what was of importance to them; it was their ability to have an impact on the organization's effectiveness through the work, and the self-directed "space" to be constantly challenged, creative, and learning. Peter Senge (1990), author of *The Fifth Discipline*, describes personal mastery this way:

> People with a high level of personal mastery live in a continual learning mode. They never "arrive." Sometimes, language, such as the term "personal mastery" creates a misleading sense of definiteness, of black

and white. But personal mastery is not something you possess. It is a process. It is a lifelong discipline. People with a high level of personal mastery are acutely aware of their ignorance, their incompetence, their growth areas. And they are deeply self-confident. Paradoxical? Only for those who do not see the "journey is the reward." (p. 142)

Again, the inner motivation comes from the journey, which is the work, the learning, the challenge, not from the outcome or the accomplishment. The completion of a task, a piece of learning, even a failure is a milestone on the journey, not an endpoint. This doesn't mean that milestones are not significant; it means that the thrill is in the ride, not in reaching the destination. Those who are focused only on the destination usually don't care about the journey, other than how fast or easy it is to get to the end. Also the sense of self-confidence, self-efficacy, makes the journey one of challenge, discovery, and fun as opposed to worrying over the pitfalls and problems, and trying to avoid any stress and difficulty.

Personal mastery is similar to the concept of professionalism. David Maister (2000, pp. 15–16) recommends these criteria for being a "true professional":

- Take pride in their work and show a personal commitment to quality.
- Reach out for responsibility.
- Anticipate and don't wait to be told what to do—show initiative.
- Do whatever it takes to get the job done.
- Get involved and don't just stick to their assigned role.
- Are always looking for ways to make things easier for those they serve.
- Are eager to learn as much as they can about the business of those they serve.
- Really listen to the needs of those they serve.
- Learn to understand and think like those they serve so they can represent them when they are not there.

- Are team players.

- Can be trusted with confidences.

- Are honest, trustworthy, and loyal.

- Are open to constructive critiques on how to improve themselves.

Professionalism is about taking pride in your work, commitment to quality, dedication to the interests of the client (be it internal or external), and a sincere desire to help. The premise of *Good Work* (Gardner et al., 2001) also speaks to professionalism but expands the concept to include ethics and social responsibility. As mentioned in Chapter Two, they define good work as "work of expert quality that benefits the broader society" (p. ix). People know they are doing good work because it feels good. This may sound too simple, but you know when the work you are doing is good and meaningful. That's why it is so important to be in touch with your inner self. It is about trusting both your judgment and your intuition. The more we know ourselves, the more we can evaluate and change our professional behavior, our moral and ethical judgment, and how our performance affects those around us.

Many people who have meaningful work and perform professionally still face tension between their desired state and their current situation. Again, to know yourself is to understand the struggle to continuously strive for more mastery. Part of that struggle is finding ways to push the boundaries of reality in order to continue to work toward your purpose.

Learning: Challenge, Creativity, and Continuous Growth

We come back to that critical aspect of meaningful work, learning. What we are doing when we are fulfilling our purpose and mastering our performance is *creating our future* (Horner, n.d.). The tension we feel in doing this can actually energize us if we see it as a challenge rather than an obstacle. Another term for this tension is stress. Although we often think of stress as something negative, it is important to remember that stress can be stimulating and helpful. Think of how boring life would be without some changes and challenges to push us along, to offer opportunities to help in learning and growing, and to give us the impetus for accomplishing our goals in life. Too little stress leads to boredom and lethargy, which is sometimes called *rustout*; too much stress leads to physical and emotional breakdown, referred to as *burnout*. The right balance of stress or tension leads to a productive, healthy life.

Another phrase that is used to convey these positive aspects is *creative tension*. This was popularized by Senge (1990) in explaining what motivates people to change. Creative tension describes the feeling people have when they recognize the difference (the gap) between their current reality and where they want to be in terms of their vision. The gap is the distance between what we have and what we want, and it creates a natural and healthy tension that seeks to resolve itself. This tension is the reason we make choices and take actions. It's the source of energy for change and the challenge that people seek in meaningful work. Unfortunately, many people are not aware of the gap because either they have no vision (purpose) or they fool themselves into believing that their reality is where they want to be. First you have to recognize that there is a gap. This is fairly easy for high performers and self-actualizers because for them there is always a gap. If you are continuously striving to reach a higher state, or your potential, then you will always be in a state of learning. Lauren Turner (2005) found in her research on learning and meaningful work that two characteristics stood out. First, learning was innately embedded in the core of each person who felt his or her work was meaningful. Second, all the people in her study were committed self-directed learners.

Study participants described the learning process as experimental, continual, iterative, messy, and cumulative. A number of them used words like *sustenance* or *fuel* to describe the role of learning in terms of their work. They also said their work would be much less meaningful if learning were not a significant part of it. They described their curiosity for learning as being a sponge; they want to soak up as much knowledge as possible. Reflection also played a critical role in their learning. They found themselves continually processing new information and questioning how it fit with their present knowledge and values. They described themselves as questioners, always wanting to know the underlying assumptions and premises that their newfound knowledge was based on. They also wanted to be able to weigh the value added for new data. In addition, they didn't tend to accept new knowledge at face value but wanted to dig deeper to learn more. Emotions were also a part of the learning process. Being aware of the thrill of discovery, struggling with new values and beliefs, and dealing with change supplied feedback and understanding. These emotions and the sense of involving their whole self in the learning actually represented a spiritual experience. Study participants verified much of what was discussed as meaningful learning in Chapter Two, even though the researcher was not exposed to the meaningful learning information at the time.

Control and Self-Directed Learning

In Chapter Two, I noted that people who seem to be in control really have coping skills and a sense of self-efficacy, as opposed to being in control (as in having power over events). The expression "knowledge is power" paradoxically is also not about having power *over* something, but having the ability to transform knowledge into understanding and ultimately wisdom. The proverbial guru on the top of the mountain is revered for his wisdom, not his power. Wisdom comes to people who are continuously learning, reflecting on what they've learned, and adjusting their worldview to help them strive to fulfill their purpose. The type of learning process that leads to a sense of control, autonomy, and empowerment is known as *self-directed learning*.

This is true because, first, the majority of professionals today are knowledge workers, and this segment of the workforce will continue to grow. Second, there is constant change and advancement in technology, and steady growth in the scope of information from multiple sources worldwide. Third, you cannot keep up with all the new knowledge just by attending formal educational courses, workshops, and the like. Even in our master's and doctoral programs, at least 30 percent of the learning, if not more, is expected to be obtained outside the classroom. Last of all, there is a tremendous amount of information and knowledge readily available through the Internet and through social networking. So the best way to learn is on your own; hence self-directed learning.

Philosophically, self-directed learning fits with the concept of self-actualization, because it is based on the notion of personal growth and striving to reach one's potential.

By taking personal responsibility for your own learning, you are controlling the learning process (Merriam, Caffarella, & Baumgartner, 2007).

Turner found that her meaningful learners were always open to any opportunity to learn something new. Learning often went on without any specific goal in mind, but simply for the sake of learning. They would pursue knowledge and understanding above and beyond what they may have needed. They are the people I described in Chapter Two who are always asking questions, always wanting to know more. They are emotional, even passionate, about learning—so they are intrinsically motivated to want to continually learn on their own. As I said earlier, learning is energy that keeps fueling meaningful work. The more you are an active self-directed learner the more you control the source and distribution of that energy.

Autonomy and Empowerment

Many, but not all, of the people who have participated in various studies on meaningful work either work for themselves or own their own business. In addition, they all report preferring to be their own boss, to have autonomy. Of those working for someone else, one of their criteria is how empowered they will be to decide how they will work, even if they do not have the power to decide what they should work on. I see autonomy as "space" or "elbow room." Do I have the autonomy to get my work accomplished the way I believe it should get accomplished?

Empowerment is the ability to exercise personal discretion or choice and transform choices into desired actions and outcomes that can have an impact on the organization or system. Autonomy is the *freedom* to exercise personal choice; empowerment is the *ability* to exercise personal choice. Both fit with the notion of control I talked about earlier. Somebody else cannot empower you anymore than that person can motivate you. Your manager and the organization can create an environment conducive to empowerment, but only you can make the choice to empower yourself. Personal mastery, self-directed learning, autonomy, and empowerment all enable you to have control over the work you do and how meaningful and fulfilling the work is for you. Even if the work itself is aligned with your purpose, you need these other elements to complete the picture.

Conclusion

If *sense of self* is about self-actualization, then the *work itself* is about its corollary, excellence. People enjoying meaningful work are really continuously striving for excellence. Since it is the work itself that is motivating, then improvement itself is motivating. A job worth doing is worth doing well.

Matthew Crawford, in his book *Shop Class as Soulcraft: An Inquiry into the Value of Work* (2009), talks about how he decided to repair motorcycles in between academic and think tank jobs. While he was working on one particularly difficult repair project, he was referred to another technician with the advice, "If anyone can help you, Fred can." Fred turned out not only to be an expert mechanic but also to have an encyclopedic knowledge of obscure European motorcycles. For someone who never went to college, Fred was a true scholar who really knew what he was doing, and who did it with integrity and joy.

4

Work-Life Balance

MANAGING THE TENSIONS

THERE IS A MYTH that work-life balance means an equal balance every day. Trying to schedule an equal number of hours for all of your various work and personal activities is usually unrewarding and unrealistic. Life is and should be more fluid; your individual work-life balance will vary over time. The right balance for you when you are single will be different from when you are married, or if you have children, or when you start a new career as opposed to when you are nearing retirement. You do need to seriously reflect on how much quality time you spend doing meaningful work, and being with your family and friends, working around the house, doing volunteer work, and relaxing. Given that most of us do not live in an ideal world, work-life balance concerns the choices we make and the tensions we have to deal with in order to have a sense of completion in our lives. No one area of our lives should dominate so much that we cease to value the other areas. All work and no play is stressful, is overwhelming, and usually results in our health, family, and social lives suffering—even if the work is meaningful. All play and no work quickly becomes boring and meaningless.

We also need to balance the nourishing of our various selves (mental, physical, emotional, and spiritual), because in the less-than-ideal world we do not have the luxury of meeting all of our needs through any one major activity. So we need to take the time to learn, keep fit, reflect, meditate or pray, and give to and be with others. Again, because we usually worry most about getting work and other responsibilities taken care of, we don't take time to care for ourselves. If we do not take care of ourselves, we cannot be there for others. So we end up running on the proverbial treadmill until we finally realize we are not meeting our own or anyone else's needs. The statistics we read in the media on work-related stress, people being overweight and less than physically fit, depression, divorce, and even workplace violence speak for themselves.

Balancing Work and the Rest of Life

The end of World War II resulted in emergence of the modern suburban family (Pruitt & Rapoport, n.d.). Soldiers and others working for the war effort returned home and got married or came back to family life during peacetime. The G.I. Bill offered former members of the military financial assistance to attend college and buy a home. Work was plentiful and centered in the emerging suburban areas around major cities. This was the start of the era of the traditional suburban family: mom and dad, two kids, a dog, and a station wagon.

Americans in the 1950s embraced stable family values in order to maintain the status quo (Russel, 1993). The fear of communism created a society craving security and conformity. So although the emerging middle class moved to the suburbs to new single-family homes, they all looked the same. Parents taught children to fit in, act normally, play by the rules. Unique or unusual behavior was viewed with suspicion. Conformity meant there was a right way of doing everything, from women learning how to cook to men learning job skills. Conformity also meant respect and obedience for authority; public schools taught patriotism, nationalism, and a proper code of behavior. "They" were the ones who knew how to do it right and could be trusted to help you learn to do it right. There were children's programs on television with authority figures, such as Captain Kangaroo, who wore a "uniform" and demonstrated how to brush our teeth. Educational civil defense programming taught us how to jump off our bikes and run for the nearest shelter if we heard the siren. The most significant programs were the ones that blatantly taught us the proper role we each had to play in the family: "Children should be seen and not heard," "Don't bother your father with your problems, he's had a rough day," "It's not proper to show your emotions in public." Also reflected were the proper roles each partner in the marriage should play, with mom staying home with the kids and dad being the "breadwinner." Academics labeled the men of the 1950s the "silent generation"; they worked for the growing corporate organizations that sold consumer goods to the suburban middle class and eventually became labeled as "organization men" (Russel, 1993).

After work, the family watched TV. "The Lone Ranger," "The Rifleman," "Roy Rogers," and other popular shows represented the frontier hero, single-handedly battling the forces of evil, and always winning. Or "Father Knows Best," "Ozzie and Harriet," and "Leave It to Beaver," which reflected the correct roles and the proper way to behave that each member of the family was expected to follow.

Then came the 1960s, with war protests, flower children and hippies, and the beginning of the women's liberation movement. Betty Friedan and other feminists started to question the traditional roles of women as homemakers and mothers. At the same time, the divorce rate began to increase, and both of these forces pushed more and more women into the workforce.

If the 1960s marked the emergence of women's lib, the 1970s were the start of the phenomenon of the dual-career couple. Given the oil crisis and inflation that ravaged the economy, many middle-class families found it more difficult than ever to get by with only one parent working, especially if they were trying to keep up with the Joneses. In 1977, a seminal work, the "Quality of Employment Survey" (Quinn & Stains), identified the problem of "work-family conflict" for the first time.

In the 1980s, more women entered the workforce and encountered the so-called glass ceiling for the first time. With the launch of *Working Mother* magazine in 1981, they also started to see the beginning of "family-friendly" policies and benefits in the workplace.

The 1990s saw these same benefits cut back as companies sought to reduce costs and increase shareholder value by downsizing and merging. The mantra at work became "do more with less"; those who were left had to do the work of those who were let go, as well as their own. In 1999, Ellen

Galinsky, president of the Families and Work Institute, wrote a book that discussed the results of a study of more than a thousand children in grades three through twelve, along with six thousand parents. On one hand, she found that more fathers were involved in parenting than twenty years earlier, and that the majority of the kids felt positive about the parenting they were receiving. On the other hand, the kids were asked if they could be granted one wish as to how their parents' work affected their lives what it would be. A significant percentage said they wished their parents would come home less stressed (or less tired). The vast majority of the parents reported having less energy to do things with their children and ignoring their children when pressured with work. The disparity between what parents said and what the kids said about the amount of quality time spent together was significant. We know the term "latchkey kid"; in the United States, a 2002 Census survey reported that 5.8 million children between the ages of five and fourteen (15 percent) who were living with a mother were caring for themselves an average of 6.3 hours per week, and 65 percent of those children spent 2 to 9 hours home alone. White non-Hispanic children are more likely to be left home alone than children of other races (Overturf, 2005).

Generations X and Y

For the first time, we have four generations represented in our workforce at the same time (Hutchings & McGuire, 2006). The baby boomer generation was born between 1946 and 1964, generation X encompasses those born from 1965 to 1980, and generation Y (or the millennials) were born after 1980. There is also the tail end of the traditional or organization-man generation still around (born prior to 1946).

Baby boomers are staying longer in the workplace rather than retiring, unlike prior generations, while their grandchildren, the millennials, are now entering the workforce. Along with this phenomenon are differences in outlook and approach between the generations. Although the aging sector of the workforce is highly experienced, work-oriented, and stable in employment, younger employees are better educated, are more mobile, exhibit less organizational commitment, are entrepreneurial, are very technologically literate, and are much more interested in work-life balance than their parents and grandparents.

The baby boomer generation accepted work-family conflict as a necessary by-product of the dual-career and single-parent work phenomena, but their children are demanding more time off to be at home. More gen Xers grew up in single-parent or dual-career families than any previous generation. They also grew up while their parents were being downsized and many companies were going out of business. According to numerous surveys, generation X and Yers report that a work schedule allowing them more time at home is one of their highest priorities in choosing a job, and fathers are spending more time at home than their dads did back in the 1980s and 1990s. Catalyst's 2001 study reported that 78 percent said flexible work policies and programs were extremely or very important to their satisfaction; they are also willing to sacrifice career or organizational advancement for a more flexible work schedule.

Probably the one characteristic that stands out above all others with the younger generation Yers is their connectivity; millennials use technology in a big way to stay in touch with each other. No previous generation has had the multitude of technological devices and communication programs that the millennials have and can use to stay in touch; from cell phones with both voice and text to MySpace and Facebook, to email and Skype. They can play video games with others around the world with Xbox Live, and they call others around the world for free with computer-based phones.

The life events that have shaped this generation include September 11, Oklahoma City, Columbine, global warming, AIDS, Katrina, Enron, the Iraq War, globalization, the digital revolution, a wildly fluctuating stock market, the rise of India and China, and an overall decline in the stature of the United States (Tapia, 2008). In the workplace, the millennials are coming of age with economic uncertainty, endless mergers and buyouts, layoffs in major industries such as automobiles, and lack of credit and other financial support systems. Millennials tend to be socially and environmentally conscious, and very pragmatic. They believe that where and when they work should not matter so long as the work gets done. Connecting, even thousands of miles away, is as easy as interacting face-to-face, and in fact even better because they can all be in more places at once. "Who I am, what I do, and the jobs and careers around me need to evolve iteratively and continuously, like software version releases. How will MyJob 1.0 evolve into MyJob 2.0? 5.3? 7.9?" (Tapia, p. 5). They know that their work arrangements are transactional and that they must be prepared to move on once the deal no longer works for them or their employer. Given uncertainty both in the workplace and in the world, many millennials place friends, family, and the community ahead of work.

CEOs and Balance

Peter Vaill once said to me that CEOs are an oppressed minority. When I asked him why, he explained that not only is it a very lonely job, but there is no work-life balance. The loneliness comes from being the only person at that level in the organization, and being ultimately accountable. The lack of work-life balance also comes from having to be available twenty-four, seven. In 2000, *Industry Week* magazine published the results of a survey of 179 CEOs concerning work-life balance; 47 percent said they would sacrifice some compensation for more personal time. Stressors that CEOs mentioned related primarily to how much time they had to spend at work (sixty plus hours a week) and the amount of traveling the position required. They reported having at best difficulty relaxing and coming home upset and grumpy, and at worst high anxiety, few long-term friendships, and ruined marriages. In a *Newsweek* article (April 4, 2005), Jack Welch, the former CEO of GE, talked about work and family:

> If there was ever a case of "Do as I say, not as I did," this is it. No one, myself included, would ever call me an authority on work-life balance. For 41 years, my operating principle was work hard, play hard and spend some time as a father. It's clear that the balance I chose had consequences for the people around me at home and at the office. For instance, my kids were raised, largely alone, by their mother, Carolyn. And from my earliest days at GE, I used to show up at the office on Saturday mornings. Not coincidentally, my direct reports showed up too. Personally, I thought these weekend hours were a blast. We would mop up the workweek in a more relaxed way and shoot the breeze about sports. I never once asked anyone,

"Is there someplace you would rather be—or need to be—for your family or favorite hobby or whatever?" The idea just didn't dawn on me that anyone would want to be anywhere but at work.

My defense, if there is one, is that those were the times. In the 1960s and '70s, all my direct reports were men. Many of those men were fathers, and fathers were different then. They did not, by and large, attend ballet recitals on Thursday afternoons or turn down job transfers because they didn't want to disrupt their kids' sports "careers." Most of their wives did not have jobs with their own competing demands. All that changed, of course.

I have dealt with dozens of work-life balance situations and dilemmas as a manager, and hundreds more as the manager of managers. And over the past three years, I've heard from many people—bosses and employees—about the complex issue of work-life balance. I have a sense of how bosses think about the issue, whether they tell you or not. You may not like their perspective, but you have to face it. There's lip service about work-life balance, and then there's reality. To make the choices and take the actions that ultimately make sense for you, you need to understand that reality: your boss's top priority is competitiveness. Of course he wants you to be happy, but only inasmuch as it helps the company win. In fact, if he is doing his job right, he is making your job so exciting that your personal life becomes a less compelling draw.

Most bosses are perfectly willing to accommodate work-life balance challenges if you have earned it with performance. The key word here is: if. Bosses know that the work-life policies in the company brochure are mainly for recruiting purposes and that real work-life arrangements are negotiated one on one in the context of a supportive culture, not in the context of, "But the company says!" People who publicly struggle with work-life balance problems and continually turn to the company for help get pigeonholed as ambivalent, entitled, uncommitted, incompetent—or all of the above.

> Even the most accommodating bosses believe that work-life balance
> is your problem to solve. In fact, most know that there are really just
> a handful of effective strategies to do that—staying focused on what
> you're doing and saying no to demands outside your work-life bal-
> ance, for example—and they wish you would use them. (p. 48)

Many executives think there is no such thing as work-life balance. They
believe that work should come before life most of the time. Although I agree
that there are days, weeks, and even portions of one's career when work may
be the most important aspect of one's life, if work becomes all consuming
then some other part of one's life will suffer. Marriages and friendships break
up, children become estranged, depression can set in, and productivity and
loyalty are lost, not gained. I read one account of a CEO who was so consumed with his work that his teenage son battered his father's car one night
because he thought it was the only way to get his attention.

Many of the CEOs interviewed for the *Industry Week* article felt that
advanced planning plays a crucial role in being able to achieve balance. The
family has to be able to have input to the CEO's calendar so those activities
become as important as business meetings. Then the CEO has to commit
to considering family and personal time as important and not to automati-
cally let business meetings and other activities trump them. CEOs also need
friends and colleagues, other people they can talk to about work issues
and friends they can relax with. Many CEOs belong to networks that come
together to share issues, learn about new leadership strategies, and socialize.
Virtually all the CEOs in the *Industry Week* survey agreed that vacations and
other breaks from work were extremely important.

Working Mothers and Balance

Raising children is an economically invisible activity. The countless hours of
unpaid effort expended in nurturing, socializing, and educating are nowhere
reflected in economists' measurements of so-called productive work. Most
women who work outside the home struggle to balance care giving with
providing the financial resources needed to maintain a family. Working
mothers experience the absence of leisure time more than anyone else in the
economy. Time-use surveys confirm that mothers in the workplace perform

the equivalent of two full-time jobs, forcing them to cut back on everything in their lives except their commitment to paid work and nurturing their children (Crittenden, 2001). Because leisure time is virtually nonexistent, the first thing they cut back on in a time crunch is housework, and then sleep. Their grueling schedules explain why so many eventually decide to give up their paychecks if they can afford to; it may be the only way they can get a good night's sleep. Employed mothers reported having six hours a week less sleep than unemployed mothers and significantly less free time. Crittenden reported that in a study of thirty-seven mothers who were working full-time, some were getting only three and a half to four and a half hours of sleep and that the participants gave up sleep and couple time rather than time spent with their children.

In *The Price of Motherhood*, Crittenden (2001) says it is widely recognized that men are doing more housework and child care than their own fathers did, particularly in households where the wife earns a significant portion of the family income. Yet the fathers are not equal contributors. Parenting activities such as caring for infants, helping with homework, studying, and reading with children remain domains in which fathers make a relatively small contribution. The same is true for household chores such as cleaning and vacuuming. Even in households where the wife earns more than half the family income, the husband will typically contribute no more than 30 percent of the domestic services and child care. Clearly, there is not complete reciprocity between most spouses. For all the changes of the last decades, one thing has remained the same: it is still women who adjust their lives to accommodate the needs of children and do what is necessary to make a home.

Gordon and Whelan (1998) discovered that women at midcareer brought personal maturity, significant professional experience, and a desire for new challenges to their work, conditions that were largely unrecognized by the organizations they studied. It is this lack of recognition and support from organizations, coupled with work, home, and individual life priorities competing for attention, that tilts the balance for these professional women to leave the workplace and seek a revitalized identity, whether by finding more fulfilling work or seeking fulfillment through their home and family life.

Dolet (2003), in her study of working mothers, described her own experience:

> At the onset of the dissertation phase of my doctoral research, I was employed by a large organization performing organization and leadership development initiatives. My son was three years old and I was four years into my second marriage. My household consisted of my son, my mother, and my husband. My son attended before and after school care and I was the sole caretaker of the home, responsible for grocery shopping, meals, laundry, and cleaning. In addition to my regular paid work, I was an adjunct professor at two institutions of higher learning. This part-time work, in addition to my regular work, doctoral research, and home life responsibilities, proved to be more than I could manage. My proverbial plate was overflowing with responsibility. I felt overwhelmed and confused. I felt exploited at home and a lack of compassion in the workplace. . . . I was well aware of the reality of my life, as well as the cultural traditions and biases that informed my desire to be a super-working mom. To that end, I began to systematically eliminate parts of myself that could possibly interfere with that role from every aspect of my life. I was an automaton at work, seldom glimpsing more than a reminiscent glimmer of the joy and excitement I once had for my work and home life. I began to question the intrinsic value of my work. I could feel myself slipping behind in my career. This bothered me since I did not want to put myself on hold. I had gained a tremendous amount of weight and felt terrible about my physical appearance. I was beginning to feel lifeless.
>
> I wondered if other women have similar experiences. I genuinely thought I should be able to have all the parts of myself fully functioning in every area of my life. I wondered how I could go back and reclaim myself and my aliveness and passion for my vocation and my home. (pp. 64–65)

Dolet's research findings on women in situations similar to hers revealed that the prevalent desire of the women she studied was to *take care of themselves within the context of taking care of others.* In most cases, they had little individual self-care time. Another major finding was that the majority of women had put their career trajectory on hold until their children were out of the nest. They had stifled their aspirations in the world of work until they felt they could give focus without taking away from their children and family time.

Working mothers tell themselves and others that they will pick up their career once their children are older and they can give more time to work. They say they would be higher-producing in their career if they did not choose to devote time to children and family. Women can have time for a second career or revitalized career after their children are out of the nest. In this sense, a working mother can have it all, over time.

Unfortunately, this also means women have to put their career on hold if they are working in one of the many organizations that don't take family needs into account. These women could have been engaged in their vocation, the meaningful work that they love. Working mothers experience a sense of loss in terms of performing at their maximum capacity in all areas of their lives. These are considerable contributions, potentially lost to the world of work and life for a huge group of talented women. Their potential is also lost before they can reclaim their whole selves. According to Edmondson Bell and Nkomo (2001), much of the literature on career and family and personal life frames the dilemma between career and personal life as an either-or choice. This premise will be discussed in more detail later in this chapter. It assumes that time and emotion can be placed in only one sphere (career or family) at a time, and that intense involvement in one area may interfere with the level of involvement in another. Dolet's study participants expressed the feeling that owing to the competing priorities in their lives they cannot at all times be all that they are, their truly authentic selves.

Career-Life Balance

Although more people are choosing careers that give them better control over their work lives, this means individuals have more responsibility for their career planning and management. They cannot rely on employers to furnish a career path and help with career planning; they have to take charge on their own and figure out where they want to go and how to get there. People may have more freedom and more options, but conversely this means a lot more risk as well. Mainero and Sullivan (2006) contend that:

> [Their] research shows that the interplay of work and family, and work and self, are inexorably intertwined. Separating out career decisions from other life decisions is a relic, an artifact of twentieth-century old-line manufacturing thinking. The media has focused only on the issue of work-family conflict by showcasing a number of high-profile women who left corporations to spend time with family, calling this a new workplace issue. But there is much more to the story. The issue affects men as well as women. [The authors] argue that it is more of a "revolt" than a revolution that is going on. . . . It is true that people, especially women, are leaving their jobs and making a statement that they are protesting against work environments that don't permit them to have a life. People are also revolting against organizations that don't permit them to be true to themselves or don't provide challenging work. Not only issues of work-family balance have ignited this change, a complex interplay among issues of authenticity, balance, and challenge is causing a workplace revolt of mass proportions. (p. 3)

Employees today are defining success on their own terms, and some are opting out of the corporate rat race. Instead of living to work, people are working to live. They are tired of the inflexibility of standard work hours and the lack of concern for work-family balance; they are leaving corporate positions in favor of more flexible career options.

Lyric Turner read an airline magazine article about "staging," the business of sprucing up homes to help them sell faster and for more money (Shaver, 2008). She had just quit a boring job with a software development government contracting firm to become a Realtor, but she craved more creativity. Two hours into a staging class, she had found her calling. "I thought, 'This is what I want to do—this is me,'" she recalls. She started her business just as the housing market was beginning to slow down and sellers were working harder to make their homes more salable. Red House Staging & Interiors now furnishes and decorates approximately five to nine vacant homes per month. Lyric also conducts up to eight consultations monthly for sellers who want to make their occupied home show better. She says she's making less than in her government contracting job, but "I'm a million times happier."

James Howard felt stagnant in his position as head painter at a large auto body repair business, and he was frustrated that his commission-based salary depended on how many cars entered the shop each week (Chang, 2008). James decided that instead of spending nine to twelve hours a day, five or six days a week in the shop, he would go to customers' houses. He created a business to fix dents, dings, and scratches at the customer's home or office, saving the car owner time and charging less than most auto body shops. Now, he is working eight hours a day, three or four days a week. By owning a business, he sets his own schedule, is home more, and can attend school events and take his sons to some of their activities.

The *Washington Post* Sunday magazine has a regular feature every week about an individual who has started a business, often after leaving a nine-to-five position. A successful career is no longer viewed as working for a single firm forever (and hasn't been for quite some time). Rather than define their lives and self-worth in terms of a preordained, often constraining career tracks, workers are creating their own "kaleidoscope careers" to suit their lives (Mainero & Sullivan, 2006). This is a career created on one's own terms, defined by one's own purpose, values, life choices, and boundaries, as opposed to a predetermined, success-based career path. Like a kaleidoscope, careers are dynamic and in motion; as one's life changes, the career journey may change as well. Younger workers will look for organizations that allow changing work and working conditions along with changing life needs.

Mainero and Sullivan found that career patterns often differed for women and men. Women tended to chose careers that provided a set of options constituting the best fit at the time, while always considering how their decisions would have an impact on other people in their lives. Men, on the other hand, often compartmentalized their lives and their careers, focusing on work first and then family, and wishing for more flexibility in the process. Men and women responded to the same career and life issues, but often in contrasting order. Men are more sequential in how they deal with life and career issues. Women are integrators, and this is why so many women are concerned about the issue of balance. Women are trying to do it all, at least some of the time, while men are doing what they must. Women and men shift and move the facets of their lives around to find the pattern that best fits their life circumstances and their own wants and needs, even if those choices defy typical definitions of career success. Mainero and Sullivan found there were three reasons women, and also men, take stock of their career decisions and make changes and transitions to meet their needs for their lives, families, and themselves. These parameters reflected:

- An individual's needs for challenge, career advancement, and self-worth, juxtaposed against

- A family's need for balance, relationships, and care giving, intersected by the person's need to say,

- "What about me? How can I be authentic, true to myself, and make genuine decisions for myself in my life?" (p. 6)

Just as a kaleidoscope uses three mirrors to create infinite patterns, kaleidoscope careerists focus on three parameters (authenticity, balance, and challenge) that combine in diverse ways throughout their lives, reflecting the unique patterns of their careers.

Another emerging phenomenon is that as people live longer they reinvent themselves, sometimes more than once, over their working life. The idea of midlife transition, which at one time was reflected in buying a sports car after the kids grew up and the family station wagon (or its contemporary equivalent, the minivan) was no longer needed, is now represented by trying on new careers that are more aligned with one's values at midlife and then again, in later years. Moving through different sets of job responsibilities, organizational settings, and even fields is not new. Being concerned with doing work that is meaningful and worthwhile—especially for the baby boomers who, initially in their careers, were more concerned with making money—is new. Most people's careers evolved through happenstance according to where the job opportunities existed (Strenger & Ruttenberg, 2008). There were pressures to make money, get ahead, and meet ego and affiliation needs. By midlife, those pressures cease to be important.

Many baby boomers also realize that what was considered by the previous generation as the "declining years" is now being thought of as equally productive years. According to a 2005 study conducted by Merrill Lynch, 76 percent of baby boomers intend to keep on working and earning through their "retirement" years—most by changing careers. Another study by MetLife Foundation/Civic Ventures found that 57 percent of Americans between the ages of fifty and seventy said they want a job that fulfills a purpose in life, while 50 percent also said they want jobs that contribute to a greater good (McKee, 2008).

Cynthia Miller (2008) did her doctoral research on how meaningful work changed over a person's working life span. The participants were ages fifty-five through eighty-one and had a minimum of twenty-five years' work experience. Her research revealed that as people moved through life, their need to make a contribution or give back to society in some way grew stronger. They wanted to be able to use the skills, strengths, and talents they had developed to serve others and make a difference in the world. They also spoke about mutual benefit: by helping others they were helping themselves; they "experienced self-fulfillment by fulfilling the needs of others" (p. 94). They also continued their self-development by helping others. A by-product of this phenomenon of mutual benefit is the number of personal relationships that were added or enhanced through helping others.

A Different Concept of Balance

When we talk about work-life balance, we are usually referring to the idea that none of the several aspects of our life (work, family, friends, and personal) should be so out of balance that it negates any of the other aspects, as with Dolet's study (2003), in which working mothers tend to ignore their own personal needs in favor of their work and family needs, or people whose jobs require a great deal of travel such that they neglect their family. As I said earlier, it is realistic to expect that day in day out, work may sometimes need to overshadow other aspects of one's life. The project with a tight deadline, a critical business trip, putting time into a demanding project to be in line for a higher position, and being responsible twenty-four, seven for people's well-being are all situations many of us have had to endure. So where's the balance?

The issue here is not how we in the West think about the concept of balance. This sense of balance is based on an either-or, win-lose type of scenario. Either I stay at work and finish the project or I go home and go to my children's soccer game. I can take this long business trip, which will enhance my chances for a promotion, but it will put an irrevocable strain on my marriage. Dilemmas of this sort leave us making choices where one area of our lives may gain something but at the expense of another. Again, I want to emphasize that I am not saying the dilemmas aren't real; the issue is how we handle them.

In Chinese philosophy, there is a concept called yin-yang (see Figure 4.1). The two sides, black and white, represent naturally opposing forces. The forces are not separated by a hard or straight line, but by a wavy line. This connotes that balance is flexible and continuous. These forces are also two sides of the same phenomenon—day and night, good and bad, young and old. Both exist at the same time and would not exist without the other. The small, opposite colored circles represent that there is a little of the opposing force in each. Using this perspective, instead of seeing myself getting older as my "declining" years, I stay young by keeping physically fit while acknowledging that my body isn't as athletic as it once was. My attitude is that there are advantages to being older, such as enjoying my seniority in the organization and not having to worry about pleasing the bosses as I thought I had to do when I was younger.

Balance can be seen as *managing tensions,* as opposed to making either-or decisions all the time. If you think of your adult life as a journey, then Vaill's permanent white water is an apt metaphor. Anyone who has been white water rafting knows that on the one hand you start out with a plan that emphasizes what the river is like, how to row, how to work together, and

---

Figure 4.1. Yin-Yang

listening to the experience of the leader at certain critical moments. On the other hand, once you are on the river there are times you need to "trust" the current and stop rowing, and there are times you have to row like crazy. Those two opposing forces aren't always predictable. You have to be flexible, willing to take risks, and trust the process and go with the flow. Work, career, and life are about managing the tensions between the need for control and the need to let go. You plan your work-life journey by identifying your values, beliefs, and purpose in life. Then you start riding, all the while knowing there will be times you will have to let go by making trade-offs or giving up control, and times you will have to be assertive about your needs. You also accept that the opposing forces of work, family, friends, and self are naturally opposing tensions that have to be managed, like managing the white water. There are two interrelated elements that can help with managing the tensions: time and energy.

Time

By now, most people know about time management: set priorities, make lists, combine chores and errands that fit together, minimize material things that you don't need and that don't add value to your life, and outsource work that others can do more cheaply and better than you can. Numerous resources can help you manage your time better. Stephan Rechtschaffen (1996), however, believes that time management is not what causes much of our tension, but instead what he calls "timeshifting." I have a saying on my office wall that I heard from a former sensitivity trainer many years ago: "We spend 90 percent of our lives either reviewing the past or rehearsing the future." I have heard it in several forms over the years. The premise of timeshifting is that we try to squeeze more out of time, as well as use technology to get more things done in less time, rather than having truly quality time. We don't know how to live in the here and now anymore; we are so busy multitasking that we don't enjoy or get any sense of satisfaction out of each task by itself. Everything just becomes something to check off as being finished. Technology has made this worse because now we can look at our email while talking on the phone about the meeting yesterday afternoon at the same time we are supposed to be watching our son's soccer game.

We think we are so efficient, and yet we fool ourselves about being such a good parent. Our children, however, are aware of what we are doing, at the same time the person at the other end of the phone conversation knows we are not giving our full attention . . . and our email recipients don't get a complete response to their queries.

Timeshifting has to do with how we spend our emotional time, how we focus on what we care about. How aware are we of what is going on at the present? I have a habit I that helps me be aware of the present when I am commuting to work. I am lucky that I don't commute on highways; I commute through residential streets and a city park. While I'm driving, I look for things I've never noticed before: the furniture on the porch of a house, the trees and bushes in the park, cars parked on the streets, new construction, and always, people walking or jogging. I have been using the same route for twenty years and am amazed how many new items I still find. Even more important, this exercises my emotional awareness and leaves me much more in the here and now for the rest of the day.

One way of restoring balance by managing the tensions is therefore to be present in everything you are doing so that you are not being pulled in different directions at the same time. One way to achieve being present is to practice *mindfulness*, a concept that is simple yet very hard to accomplish. It is supposed to have originated with Buddhist meditation. Mindfulness is a way to keep your attention in the present moment. The goal is simply to observe, with no intention of changing or improving anything. Mindfulness supports living each and every moment to the fullest. It is an attitude about life as well as a relaxation technique. Mindfulness is a means of observing and accepting what is occurring at the moment, and accepting life just as it is right now, with all its positives and negatives. If used in a conversation, you listen with your whole attention focused on the speaker and are not worrying about getting your opinion or reaction out. When mindfulness is used while observing, then all five senses are brought to bear on what you are observing (rather than where you are going next). Mindfulness often leads to increased confidence, a calmer mood, and enhanced coping skills. It can help you feel more rooted in who you are, what your purpose is, and where you are going in life. It's a way of stopping the action and grounding yourself.

Energy

We have all had times when life was coming at us so fast we were surviving on half-eaten meals, racing from one appointment or meeting to another, gulping down coffee to stay awake, and falling into bed only to hear the alarm go off so we can go through the same process again. Even when we are not racing, most of us act as if time is of the essence. When everything is not going as efficiently as possible, we grow irritable, depressed, and anxious, and our energy is sapped.

According to Loehr and Schwartz (2003), energy is the critical element of high performance. They believe there are four sources of energy: physical, emotional, mental, and spiritual. They are all interrelated, affecting our ability to work to our potential. It's hard to focus (mental) if you didn't sleep enough the night before (physical), you had a fight with your spouse in the morning (emotional), and you have been struggling with the morality of your company's trying to freeze out a competitor by cutting off their distribution channel (spiritual). Just as muscles need recovery time after heavy exertion, so do we after other types of energy exertion. We have all experienced fatigue after an emotionally draining experience. Muscles need to be pushed beyond their limit in order to grow stronger, and so do the other forms of energy. We now know that continued mental stimulation keeps the brain rejuvenated well into our later years.

Taking care of ourselves has to do with feeding all four types of energy, stretching their limits in healthy ways, and taking the time to cool down. We all know what we need to do to keep physically fit. To develop our emotional capacity, we require fulfilling relationships with people who care about us but also challenge us to expand our emotional capacity. We must also be aware and live our values and beliefs (spiritual), and pursue learning activities that stretch our intellectual muscles.

Conclusion

Work-life balance has to do with being anchored by a foundation of purpose and meaning, while remaining flexible enough to bend with changing needs and conditions. Integration comes from bringing the whole self to whatever you are doing and then focusing on what you are doing, be it work or play.

Annie McKee (2008) is an executive coach who works with numerous executives struggling with work-life balance. Max, one of her clients, recounted:

> My daughter came home from camp this summer, and I almost didn't recognize her. She's twelve, and honestly, she looks and acts like a teenager. Where did my little girl go? Got me thinking, you know? Soon she'll be eighteen, and she'll be gone. So this summer I've tried to spend a lot more time with her. But it just isn't working. It breaks my heart, because I know it's my fault. All these years, all the travel, the meetings, the deadlines. . . . I just wasn't around. I missed her plays and her games and even her birthdays. . . . My wife took care of all that so well, I thought we'd be fine. But we aren't. I don't know her, and she doesn't know me. She doesn't really want to be around me. We can't even have a decent conversation, and it's so clear that she isn't having fun when I try to do things with her. I've lost her.

On top of this, his job was falling apart and he had just missed a promotion. He was missing a lot at home, sleeping poorly, and having far too many small but troubling arguments with his wife. He worked longer and later, stopped seeing close friends, and couldn't really relax or unplug.

Gradually, Max started imagining the full life he wanted most at home and at work. The change began slowly. He went to his daughter's soccer games, simply showing up with no expectations of her—just of himself—wanting only to be a true supportive presence in her life. After a while, they started biking the few miles to the games together and chatting a bit along the way. At the same time, he and his wife agreed to take walks every Sunday together—no talking, just being together. It didn't take long before they felt comfortable with each other once again, open enough to share their thoughts, their frustrations, and their hopes for their family.

Change didn't happen for Max only at home; he approached work differently as well. Every single morning he found time to close his door for ten minutes and simply reflect. He focused optimistically on the day before and on the day ahead, and he became adept at thinking about the challenges, problems, and solutions without letting the stress throw him. Instead of eating on the run every day, he began inviting a direct report or another team member to join him for lunch several times a week. By spending more and better time with the people in his life, he slowly reawakened his own passion for his career as he rebuilt his connection with his family.

Meaningful Workplaces

5

The Elements of a
Meaningful Workplace

RECENTLY, ORGANIZATIONS have been attempting to attract and
retain highly qualified workers in advance of a projected labor shortage and amid increasing global competition. These new employees have
expressed a preference to work for socially responsible, ethically driven organizations that allow the whole self to be brought to work. According to the
Society for Human Resource Management's 2008 Workplace Forecast report
(SHRM, 2008b), four of the ten key themes identified are:

1. The implications of increased global competitiveness, especially the
    need for an educated and skilled workforce

2. Demographic changes, especially the aging of the workforce, the
    impending retirement of the baby boom generation, and greater
    demand for work-life balance

3. Growing need to develop retention strategies for current and future
    workforce

4. Demographic shifts leading to a shortage of high-skilled workers

Other relevant findings from their survey include:

- Growth in the number of *employees with caring responsibilities* (elder care, child care, elder care and child care at the same time)

- Generational issues, recognizing and *catering to groups* such as generation Y (born 1980–2000), generation X (born 1965–1980), and so on

At the time this book was written, the United States and the rest of the world were going through a chaotic economic decline, and even before the economic turmoil fully emerged employees in an SHRM study on job satisfaction identified job security as their top concern (SHRM, 2008a). The rest of the top four are benefits, compensation, and feeling safe in the work environment. The top four contributors to job satisfaction are actually *not satisfiers*, according to Herzburg, but basic hygiene factors or lower-order elements in Maslow's hierarchy. They were rated high at least in part because of the dismal economic situation. To call them contributors to satisfaction, or motivational factors, is a misnomer.

Five of the top ten contributors to job satisfaction are motivational:

1. Opportunities to use skills and abilities
2. Relationship with immediate supervisor
3. The work itself
4. Meaningfulness of job
5. Flexibility to balance life and work issues

What all these findings point to is a desire among the American workforce to be part of an organization that is going to take care of them and help them take care of their family, support their growth through skill and knowledge development, understand their need to have some work-life balance, and use their skills and abilities meaningfully. The American Business Collaboration for Quality Dependent Care conducted an earlier study that identified these same findings. This organization is a consortium of seven Fortune 500 companies that have partnered to ensure their employees have access to quality programs and services to help them manage their work and personal responsibilities (WFD Consulting, 2006). The study found that although there were differences in terms of age and gender, a competitive compensation package, even if important, is not enough to attract today's most valued employees. Organizations competing for critical talent must take a total-rewards approach by looking beyond salary to pinpoint the actual priorities of these individuals. Whenever possible, companies should customize opportunities for their critical talent pool, offering a package of tangible and intangible incentives rooted in what is important in an employee's professional and personal life.

Great Workplaces

In 1988, Robert Levering and Milton Moskowitz wrote *The 100 Best Companies to Work for in America,* a book based on six years of research about the elements of great work environments. Levering attributes his interest in pursuing the inquiry in part to Peters and Waterman's work on identifying the elements of excellent companies, *In Search of Excellence* (1982). According to Levering, Peters and Waterman's book represented a departure in how organizations tended to be analyzed and judged. Until then, productivity was considered a result of efficient use of resources, and effectiveness was measured in terms of profit and stock dividends. *In Search of Excellence* identified elements concerned with how a company was managed, especially in terms of its people. Instead of ending with productivity and profits, they started with eighteen companies considered leaders of their market segments and looked at what they had in common that stood out as contributing factors to their success. What Peters and Waterman did for management practice and work processes, Levering and Moskowitz did for the work environment and organizational culture.

The notion of being identified as a great place to work was quickly recognized by leaders in a variety of economic sectors as a prime means to improve their organizational effectiveness, and their image to both potential employees and the general public.

Their book eventually led to an annual project conducted by the Great Place to Work Institute approximately fifteen years ago: to identify the top one hundred companies to work for, based on work-life programs, humanistic values, and social responsibility. After several years, *Fortune* magazine picked up sponsorship of the list (although the project is still conducted by the same institute) and in turn spawned several other similar programs sponsored by magazines catering to population groups such as *Working Mother* magazine and *AARP* magazine. City magazines, such as *Washingtonian*, and other municipal and state entities, such as Minnesota Work-Life Champions and (what was then called) the Maryland Work-Life Alliance, also sponsor similar lists. The ongoing theme of all these projects has been concern for the human in the organization and reaction to prioritizing profits over people. Handy (2002) said that enlightened companies exist not just to make a profit but to do something better, more useful, or of higher quality than other organizations. A theme echoed by Collins and Porras (1994) in *Built to Last* is that those companies that have "stood the test of time" have as a basis for their mission creating something of value for society, and their core values and purpose constitute a solid foundation. According to Jeffery Pfeffer of Stanford University, "Companies that treat people right get enormous dividends: high rates of productivity, low rates of turnover. Companies that treat people poorly experience the opposite—and end up complaining about the death of loyalty and the dearth of talent" (Pfeffer, 1998).

Levering (2000) further investigated what elements made the companies that were selected for the "100 Best Companies to Work for" list so desirable as workplaces. He visited 125 companies in thirty states and talked with hundreds of employees about their workplaces. Levering then revisited twenty especially good workplaces for further interviews with lower-level employees, top officers, and founders. He also reviewed the data from the employee questionnaires that were anonymously submitted as part of the application packet. The same five phrases were heard over and over: "A friendly place," "There isn't much politics around here," "You get a fair shake," "It's just like family," and "It's more than a job." From these interviews, a definition was created: "A great workplace is one in which you trust the people you work for, have pride in what you do, and enjoy the people you are working with" (Levering, p. 26). He labeled the elements of a great workplace culture as *credibility, respect, fairness, pride,* and *camaraderie.*

Findings from the Study

I wanted to dig deeper to find out how organizations achieve these attributes. I had been a "judge" for two years for the Maryland Work-Life Alliance, which annually recognized organizations (profit, nonprofit, government, and associations) for their support for work-life programs for their employees. The organizations had either to be based in Maryland or to constitute a significant presence in the state.

The alliance had been awarding its "seal of excellence" for five years when this study was undertaken. The list of awardees included such organizations as Discovery Communications, Marriott International, SAS Institute, MITRE Corporation, Booz Allen Hamilton, National Oceanographic and Atmospheric Agency, and Calvert Mutual Funds, as well as banks, hospitals, technology firms, and municipal governments. This list is noteworthy in that it included national and local government organizations, nonprofits, and associations, as well as national and international corporations. Of the fifty-seven winners of the award, we identified seventeen to participate in our study, and ten agreed to interviews. We conducted personal or telephone interviews with human resource management representatives, as well as analyzing their written submissions for this award. Several companies are also on *Fortune* magazine's 100 Best Companies to Work For list and the *Washingtonian* magazine's 50 Best Places to Work For list. In addition, we examined not only their work-life programs and policies but also their programs and policies on social responsibility, philanthropy, and community service.

Living a Values-Based Culture

First, we found there was a strong values-based culture present in each of the organizations. This was evident by the overwhelming alignment between the organization's mission and its commitment to the employees, customers, suppliers, and community. At Marriott the motto is "the spirit to serve" ("There is a 'Marriott Way.' It's about serving the associates, the customer, and the community. Marriott's fundamental beliefs are enduring and the keys to its continued success."). At Sandy Spring Bank, a small Maryland-based financial institution, community banking isn't just a slogan. Its commitment is to help communities be better places to live and work, as well as building internal workplace communities.

In addition, we found that development of employees was one of the values embedded in the culture, not just an add-on. An example statement: "At Booz Allen, we're very serious about our responsibility for developing our people. We help our people realize their potential and fulfill their ambitions by helping them shape their own individual career paths. From mentoring to off-site courses and from on-the-job learning to mining our award-winning knowledge networks, we provide the tools needed for our people to develop world-class analytical, leadership, management, and relationship-building skills." At Discovery Communications the "goal of enabling consumers to explore their world and satisfy their curiosity depends on maintaining a creative and entrepreneurial environment where individual expression, achievement and recognition go hand-in-hand with our business objectives and performance."

The commitment to diversity is the same as the commitment to learning; it is not a separate program, but an integral part of the culture and the practice of everyday work life. At MITRE Corporation, there is a Corporate Diversity Awareness Committee that is employee-run and has the full support of management. Every other organization we interviewed had the same or similar committees and activities that were employee-run.

Caring About Employees

A second theme we found is that the organizations have a strong employee focus. This is illustrated by how they treat their employees as assets—as true "associates." At software maker SAS Institute, "If you treat employees as if they make a difference to the company, they will make a difference to the company." SAS has been featured on "60 Minutes" as having an extensive set of work-life benefits. Yet employees say they would still work for the company even without all the benefits.

Most of the organizations conduct periodic internal employee satisfaction audits, and cross-functional employee teams develop action agendas based on the results. Most of the work-life policies and programs are generated through these action teams, through employee forums, or simply from employee requests. One story from Calvert Mutual Funds exemplifies the commitment to work-life. Employees asked the company to support use of public transportation by subsidizing fares; many other metropolitan-based organizations offer this benefit as well. At Calvert, the employees who commuted by bicycle felt they were entitled to a subsidy. So the company contributed to the cost of their bicycles. Not to be left out, the walkers asked for support. So the company subsidized the cost of their shoes.

An interesting balance to this perspective on employees is that it is matched by an equally serious commitment to hold managers accountable for creating and nurturing a caring and supportive environment for employees. At Choice Hotels, managers are expected to be out with the employees working side-by-side. Hands-on management means taking care of employees as if they were extended family. Executives and managers living the culture lead all these organizations. There is an overall feeling that if you want to be a successful manager in any of these organizations you must model the organization's values.

Caring About the Organizational Mission

NOAA interviewees talked about the tremendous pride in the mission and in the work that is evident in the quality of their services and in their involvement in the community and society at large. MITRE's management and employees talk about commitment to the highest possible quality in products and services. At all the organizations we interviewed, empowerment and integrity went hand-in-hand with pride. At Booz Allen, "you [the employee] create your own destiny and carve out your individual path. You are the driver and the firm is here to help." At SAS, the emphasis is on intrinsic motivation and trusting people to do a good job. Knowledge workers want to push the envelope, which is encouraged at SAS. All these organizations hire talented people, give them a mission they can be proud of, and then get out of their way.

Work, Play, and Community Involvement

Finally, the organizations all describe a culture where everyone works hard and plays hard. Employees find their work to be meaningful, and they believe in the mission of the organization. They also enjoy socializing with their colleagues because of the sense that "we're all in this together." At most of the organizations, employee groups organized the social activities, with management support and participation. The diversity-based groups also organized social and educational activities, and organizations used holidays and other occasions to celebrate the organizational community.

The sense of community and social responsibility was overwhelming. Calvert gives up to twelve paid days per year for volunteer work. NOAA employees lend their expertise to helping with cleanup of the Chesapeake Bay. Sandy Spring Bank has an in-school banking program to help kids learn how to save and manage their money. These organizations spend time and money thinking about and implementing ways to serve their communities. Social responsibility was an integral part of their organizational culture, not just a nice thing to do or merely pursued for public relations value.

The next three chapters elaborate and expand on this research by discussing the elements of a meaningful workplace:

- Values-based organizational cultures, including leadership and work-life issues

- Social responsibility and diversity

- Engagement and commitment, and the workplace as community

6

Values-Based Organizational Culture

I think many people assume, wrongly, that a company exists simply to make money. While this is an important result of a company's existence, we have to go deeper and find the real reasons for our being. As we investigate this, we inevitably come to the conclusion that a group of people get together and exist as an institution that we call a company so that they are able to accomplish something collectively that they could not accomplish separately—they make a contribution to society, a phrase which sounds trite but is fundamental.

—David Packard, cofounder of Hewlett Packard, 1939

ACCORDING TO COLLINS AND PORRAS (1994) the first question a new CEO should ask after walking through the door is not, "What needs to change?" but *"What do we stand for and why do we exist?"* (p. xiv; emphasis added). Organizations that put profits before people (their employees) tend not to last long. Organizations that take a balanced view of the needs of their employees, customers, and other stakeholders can and will be profitable, all other things being equal. In a white paper produced by British Telecommunications, the CEO of BT Retail at the time, Pierre Danon wrote: "Running a business is always a balancing act . . . some may interpret [this paper] as a framework for business excellence, others as a business case for corporate social responsibility, and others as a recipe for improved customer satisfaction. We see it as all three" (Danon, 2001, p. 1). The paper goes on to discuss the concept of *stake*holder value rather than *share*holder value. As Collins and Porras point out (2002), profits are to companies as breathing is to humans. We need to breathe to live, but our purpose in life is not to breathe. Likewise, companies need to make a profit to survive, but making a profit is not a relevant purpose or value of a sustainable company.

Somehow, the concept of shareholder value as a goal has led American companies to disregard the means by which an organization achieves such a goal, according to Charles Handy (2002). Certainly the recession that we experienced as of 2008 was initiated in part by the goal of profits and executive compensation above all else by various financial institutions. This is what happens when companies lose sight of what is critical to building an organizational culture that takes into account all the stakeholders in growing a sustainable (and profitable) organization. Handy actually considered the title of his essay, "What's a Business for?" as a moral question. In fact, satisfaction of all the stakeholders of an organization should be a moral imperative. As Danon's white paper points out, happy employees lead to happy customers and happy customers lead to happy shareholders. In turn, happy shareholders (including executives) lead to happy employees. In addition, companies have a larger responsibility to the society in which they exist. Gone are the days of dumping toxic wastes in local rivers and using lead paint on toys, at least in most developed countries; corporate social responsibility is no longer a fad. To be sustainable, an organization must take into account its relationship to the suppliers, distributors, community, and planet.

These are the kinds of issues that a values-based culture is all about. Values-based organizations practice leadership and management through shared productive and ethical human values (Harung, 1999). Within this broad framework, self-managing individuals will demonstrate a high level of meaning, enthusiasm, initiative, creativity, integrity, happiness, and self-organization—for the benefit of themselves and their organizations. Such organizations value their employees as their greatest assets.

Just as an individual should be guided through life by purpose and foundational values and beliefs, so too should an organization. The eighteen companies Collins and Porras studied all stayed true to their core purpose and values.

In fact, this became a critical aspect of their findings. Simply put, organizational culture is the representation of the purpose and values of the organization portrayed through the behavior and words of its leaders and employees. It includes the stated vision and mission, public relations communications, the quality of products and services, internal policies and procedures, and even the working environment. But most important, it is how managers and employees behave day to day that is the most revealing aspect of culture—what is often called "walking the talk." Espousing a values-based culture is one thing; living it is another. Organization culture, much like societal culture, tends to grow more entrenched as the organization matures. There is an interesting paradox about culture that vexes executives and consultants alike. Strong values and purpose result in a strong culture, which results in a clear focus about such issues as what kind of people fit in terms of hiring and certain customs and procedures that are unwritten but closely followed. Strong cultures are also the hardest to change when change is needed. Cameron and Quinn (2006) reported that as many as three-quarters of major change efforts fail, and the most frequently cited reason was a problem with the organizational culture. Collins and Porras found that values and purpose can and should remain strong as long as the strategies and operating practices remain flexible.

What Goes into a Values-Based Culture

Corporations that put people before profits outperform businesses whose primary goal is to make money. In high-performing, values-based organizations the first priority is satisfaction of employees and customers. These organizations have substantially less absenteeism and less turnover, more innovation, and higher profits and return on investment. In fact, from January 1, 1926, until December 31, 1990, the average return on investment for the stock in the eighteen visionary, high-performing companies investigated by Collins and Porras grew more than fifteen times the general U.S. stock market. Ultimately, the importance of a company's reputation within the wider society is an indication of how well it serves society, in terms of the quality and usability of its products and services, success in attracting and retaining talented employees, and the lasting value of its stock.

Values-Based Leadership

Traditionally, the practice of leadership in organizations runs the gamut from outright dictatorial to directive to benevolently paternalistic to collegial. Most approaches to leadership start with the premise that leaders should lead. This sounds obvious, and it is true that leaders are held accountable for the success of their unit, department, or the whole organization. But this premise also assumes that employees need to be led, and this brings up McGregor's famous Theory X and Theory Y (1960). As a refresher:

- Theory X: management's role is to coerce and control employees.
  - People have an inherent dislike for work and will avoid it whenever possible.
  - People must be coerced, controlled, directed, or threatened with punishment in order to get them to achieve the organizational objectives.
  - People prefer to be directed, do not want responsibility, and have little or no ambition.
  - People seek security above all else.
- Theory Y: management's role is to develop the potential in employees and help them release that potential toward common goals.
  - Work is as natural as play and rest.
  - People will exercise self-direction if they are committed to the objectives.
  - People learn to accept and seek responsibility.
  - Creativity, ingenuity, and imagination are widely distributed among the population; people are capable of using these abilities to solve an organizational problem.
  - People have potential and want to grow.

I want to believe we are way past the era of Theory X, although I know there are managers and leaders who still approach their employees on this basis. I also want to believe that most leaders want to help their organizations be successful, and they have every intention to be a Theory Y boss, but they get stuck in the power-and-control mode because they feel it's the only way to ensure they will be accountable. There are also leaders who just love to have power and control, and no matter what their intentions they are inclined to behave in a Theory X fashion.

Values-based leadership arises from Theory Y in terms of Maslow's and McGregor's beliefs that people want to develop their potential and are motivated primarily by intrinsic values. One way to manage Theory Y employees is to *serve* rather than lead.

> True leaders are hardly known to their followers.
> Next best are leaders who are loved.
> Next those who are feared.
> And the worst are those they despise.
> To give no trust.
> Is to get no trust.
> When the work is done well,
> The people say:
> "We did it ourselves." (Le Guin, 1997, p. 17)

Two contemporary concepts, *servant leadership* and *stewardship*, fit one of the oldest of all descriptions of leadership (above, cited in Le Guin) from the Tao Te Ching (sixth century B.C.). Both speak to the idea of serving rather than directing. (The idea is embodied in the expression "the wind beneath my wings," the title of Bette Midler's Grammy-winning song.)

Servant leadership (Greenleaf, 1970) is a way of being that seeks to involve others in problem solving and decision making, emphasizes ethical and caring behavior, and enhances employees' personal growth while supporting organizational work-life benefits. Some consider the more popular concept of transformational leadership to be similar to servant leadership. Transformational leadership (Burns, 1978) involves both the leader and follower acting to improve one another's lives. Specifically, these leaders focus on the higher-level needs of others (esteem, self-fulfillment, self-actualization). Although transformational leadership aligns with the same philosophical foundation as servant leadership, the focus on the serving is to the organization rather than the individual (Stone, Russell, & Patterson, 2004). Servant leaders serve their employees because they believe that satisfied and self-actualized employees will ultimately benefit the organization. They have a strong desire to help others achieve and grow. Servant leaders tend to shun attention or accolades; they lead in a supportive role rather than a directive or charismatic one. Greenleaf believed that servant leaders tend to emerge as the instrumental force in a group and then come to the attention of leaders who are enlightened enough to recognize their strength.

Larry Spears (2002), the former CEO of the Greenleaf Center, identified ten characteristics of servant leaders:

1. *Listening* Leaders have traditionally been valued for their communication and decision-making skills. Although these are also important skills for the servant-leader, they need to be reinforced by a deep commitment to listening intently to others. The servant-leader seeks to identify the will of a group and helps to clarify that will. He or she listens receptively to what is being said and unsaid. Listening also encompasses getting in touch with one's own inner voice. Listening, coupled with periods of reflection, are essential to the growth and well-being of the servant-leader.

2. *Empathy* The servant-leader strives to understand and empathize with others. People need to be accepted and recognized for their special and unique spirits. One assumes the good intentions of co-workers and colleagues and does not reject them as people, even when one may be forced to refuse to accept certain behaviors or performance. The most successful servant-leaders are those who have become skilled empathetic listeners.

3. *Healing* The healing of relationships is a powerful force for transformation and integration. One of the great strengths of servant-leadership is the potential for healing one's self and one's relationship to others. Many people have broken spirits and have suffered from a variety of emotional hurts. Although this is a part of being human, servant leaders recognize that they have an opportunity to help make whole those with whom they come in contact.

4.   *Awareness* General awareness, and especially self-awareness, strengthens the servant-leader. Awareness helps one in understanding issues involving ethics, power, and values. It lends itself to being able to view most situations from a more integrated, holistic position. As Greenleaf observed: "Awareness is not a giver of solace—it is just the opposite. It is a disturber and an awakener. Able leaders are usually sharply awake and reasonably disturbed. They are not seekers after solace. They have their own inner serenity."

5.   *Persuasion* Another characteristic of servant-leaders is a reliance on persuasion, rather than on one's positional authority, in making decisions within an organization. The servant-leader seeks to convince others, rather than coerce compliance. This particular element offers one of the clearest distinctions between the traditional authoritarian model and that of servant-leadership. The servant-leader is effective at building consensus within groups. This emphasis on persuasion over coercion finds its roots in the beliefs of the Religious Society of Friends (Quakers)—the denominational body to which Robert Greenleaf belonged.

6.   *Conceptualization* Servant-leaders seek to nurture their abilities to dream great dreams. The ability to look at a problem or an organization from a conceptualizing perspective means that one must think beyond day-to-day realities. For many leaders, this is a characteristic that requires discipline and practice. The traditional leader is consumed by the need to achieve short-term operational goals. The leader who wishes to also be a servant-leader must stretch his or her thinking to encompass broader-based conceptual thinking. Servant-leaders are called to seek a delicate balance between conceptual thinking and a day-to-day operational approach, which executives and managers must also practice effectively.

7.   *Foresight* Closely related to conceptualization, the ability to foresee the likely outcome of a situation is hard to define, but easier to identify. One knows foresight when one experiences it. Foresight is a characteristic that enables the servant-leader to understand the lessons

from the past, the realities of the present, and the likely consequence of a decision for the future. It is also deeply rooted within the intuitive mind. Foresight remains a largely unexplored area in leadership studies, but one most deserving of careful attention.

8. *Stewardship* Robert Greenleaf's view of all institutions was one in which CEOs, staffs, and trustees all played significant roles in holding their institutions in trust for the greater good of society. Servant leadership, like stewardship, assumes first and foremost a commitment to serving the needs of others. It also emphasizes the use of openness and persuasion, rather than control.

9. *Commitment to the growth of people* Servant-leaders believe that people have an intrinsic value beyond their tangible contributions as workers. As such, the servant-leader is deeply committed to the growth of each and every individual within his or her organization. The servant-leader recognizes the tremendous responsibility to do everything in his or her power to nurture the personal and professional growth of employees and colleagues. In practice, this can include (but is not limited to) concrete actions such as making funds available for personal and professional development, taking a personal interest in the ideas and suggestions from everyone, encouraging worker involvement in decision-making, and actively assisting laid-off employees to find other positions.

10. *Building community* The servant-leader senses that much has been lost in recent human history as a result of the shift from local communities to large institutions as the primary shaper of human lives. This awareness causes the servant leader to seek to identify some means for building community among those who work within a given institution. Servant-leadership suggests that true community can be created among those who work in businesses and other institutions. Greenleaf said, "All that is needed to rebuild community as a viable life form for large numbers of people is for enough servant leaders to show the way, not by mass movements, but by each servant leader demonstrating his or her unlimited liability for a quite specific community-related group." (pp. 2–5)

The eighth characteristic, stewardship, is also the title of a book on leadership by Peter Block (1993). Block sees stewardship as an organizational philosophy where leaders value service over control. This includes shared vision, power, and accountability; commitment to the larger organizational community rather than to oneself; and more equitable distribution of rewards. Block goes on to make a bold statement about the need to radically change our mind-set about leadership. Much as servant leadership requires a shift in viewing the leader as being *over* people, stewardship requires a shift in the leader being *responsible* for people and for the work.

To state it bluntly, strong leadership does not have within itself the capability to create the *fundamental changes* our organizations require. It is not the fault of the people in these positions; it is the fault of how we have framed the role. Our search for strong leadership in others expresses a desire for others to assume ownership and responsibility for our group, our organization, and our society (Block, 1993). Leadership can, and should, be seen as a critical but equal role to the other technical, administrative, and professional roles in an organization. The leader as servant or steward is a supporting, coordinating, facilitating role that does not require power and control. In fact, the leader as facilitator and coach allows ownership and responsibility to be shared so that everyone feels empowered to contribute to the mission and vision of the organization. Because power and control are shared, meaningfulness can more easily emerge for all.

Men's Wearhouse: An Example of Servant Leadership

Men's Wearhouse, a retail clothing chain, has been developing servant leaders for its offices and stores for many years.

> We have long had an intuitive sense that the key to choosing leaders lies in looking for people who enjoy helping others learn, achieve, and grow as people. Why? Because it feels like the right way to build a company. And because it's good for business. We have always known that a store or office team will trust and respect a manager who is authentically concerned about their welfare and development. Mentoring takes time and effort. Leaders who naturally care about their team will take the time to provide specific feedback and

direction—day after day. We recognize that individuals will make mistakes, but those mistakes are a necessary part of learning. Leaders must also care enough to have the "straight talk" conversations that are needed when employees are not honoring their commitment to learn. Because servant leadership is at the core of our management philosophy, our policies arise naturally out of the perspective of serving our teammates as well as our customers. We try to provide an environment that inspires, encourages, and supports the progress of our current and emerging servant leaders.

- On the way to work, a supervisor stops by a sick employee's house to drop off his paycheck—along with a direct deposit form—and find out how he's doing.

- A field operations trainer stays late to close out the store so the assistant manager can leave early to spend time with his high school age daughter who is competing in the statewide debating championships the next day.

- A regional manager stays up all night—along with the entire store team—to scan inventory and hang up product for a new store's grand opening the next day.

Over time, servant leaders naturally emerge within a group and gain the respect and trust of the people around them. And we look for that unfolding. That's why we recognize the value of promoting from within. We would rather promote someone we know, someone who has demonstrated the characteristics of a servant leader—even if he or she has not managed before. (Men's Wearhouse website, http://employment.menswearhouse.com:80/ats/advantageSelector .action?type=culture)

Authenticity, discussed in Chapter Two, also applies to leaders as well as other individuals in organizations. According to George, Sims, McLean, and Mayer (2007), "Authentic leaders demonstrate a passion for their purpose, practice their values consistently, and lead with their hearts as well as their heads. They establish long-term, meaningful relationships and have the self-discipline to get results. They know who they are" (p. 1). The authors go on to discuss the results of their research on leaders that found *no common charac-teristics* as to what constitutes good leadership. What they did find is that authentic leaders are constantly testing themselves through real-world experi-ences and reframing their worldview to challenge and understand their values and beliefs. In doing so, they discover what they stand for as leaders and that their authenticity is the source of their effectiveness. Again, as discussed in Chapter Two, meaningful learners also constantly seek to understand their purpose and value their personal awareness. Authentic leaders seek to not only bring their whole selves to work but also strive to be authentic in all aspects of their lives—with family, friends, volunteer work, and in other activities. Their authenticity is not something they wear when needed, like a winter coat. Their lives are integrated in terms of being themselves in all aspects of their lives. Just as important, they support and value those around them (their employees) who are also authentic.

When leaders truly value their employees, they are fulfilling a moral imperative to believe in human potential. This attitude reflects Maslow and McGregor's theories and also the simple truth of what is known as the Pygmalion Effect, named after the original play from which *My Fair Lady* was adapted. Just as Eliza Doolittle rose from a flower girl to being passed off as a duchess, numerous research studies have shown that people will rise to the positive expectations set by their leaders (parents, teachers, and managers). If leaders expect high performance from their employees and communicate that expectation, they increase the likelihood of getting high performance. Maybe a more appropriate term for the kind of leader this section is describ-ing is *enabler*, one who allows others to grow and perform to their highest capacity, with work that is meaningful and fulfilling, in an organization that is supportive and caring.

The Business Case for Values-Based Cultures

The Families and Work Institute conducted a national study in 1997 that found the *quality* of workers' jobs and the *supportiveness* of their workplace are the most significant predictors of job satisfaction, commitment to their employer, and retention. Job and workplace characteristics are far more important than pay and benefits (which are generally competitive with the marketplace). In fact, the research delved deeper into the work environment and discovered that it is actually a significant source of employees' problems. In other words, at those workplaces that are unsupportive and have overly demanding jobs, employees tend to carry their stress home. In fact, it creates a vicious cycle of work stress, spillover into personal and family life, and more stress back at work. In two reports on work-life initiatives, the institute (2007, 2008) identified examples of tangible benefits to organizations that have, at the least, elements of a values-based culture.

> Before 1988, Aetna experienced 23 percent turnover among employees who were new mothers following childbirth. The company found that those most likely to leave were their highest performers. In response, Aetna extended its parental leave to six months, allowed a part-time return to work, and trained supervisors in managing leaves. The company found that turnover was reduced by half, to between 9 and 12 percent. Aetna calculated savings at approximately $1 million per year.

> A study conducted of Fel-Pro, an automotive gasket company with many work-life benefits, headquartered in Skokie, Illinois, found that those who used the most benefits at Fel-Pro had the highest performance evaluations and the lowest intention of leaving the company. Furthermore, they had fewer disciplinary actions against them. Fel-Pro also found that the beneficial effects of a supportive culture go beyond traditional indicators of productivity. The greater workers' use of benefits, the greater their citizenship behavior at work, as seen in helping co-workers and supervisors, volunteering for work, and showing initiative. Perhaps most significant in this time of rapid organizational change, the workers who use and appreciate Fel-Pro's benefits are more likely to positively participate in and support changes taking place in the company. These workers show greater participation in teams and more problem solving, and they are twice as likely to submit suggestions for product and process improvements.

> Johnson & Johnson's evaluation of its comprehensive work-life programs found that introduction of flexible work policies and dependent

care programs had a measurable effect on reducing work-life conflict; it also fostered loyalty to the company. However, more influential even than programs was the work environment, as reflected in employees' assessment of supervisor support and company culture. Workers with supportive supervisors, and those who believe that the company is supportive of their family and personal needs, feel less stressed, feel more successful in balancing work and family life, are more loyal to the company, are more likely to recommend J&J as a place to work, and are more satisfied with their jobs.

In the call center industry (with a 40 percent turnover rate), the Continental Airlines Reservations Department in Houston has two thousand employees but keeps its annual turnover at 5 percent. They accomplish this, in part, by having six hundred reservation agents working from home, which has the added benefit of supporting Mayor Bill White's "Flex in the City" initiative to reduce traffic congestion and air pollution and increase business productivity. Continental's Expanded Day Off shift program also gives 25 percent of its staff three or more days off every week on a rotating basis. Flex in the City reports positive results as well: during the two-week period when results were measured in 2007, commuters spent approximately fifteen minutes less in commuting time per trip, resulting in saved time and money.

First Tennessee, headquartered in Memphis, puts employees first. This core business strategy was adopted following research demonstrating that the bank's most profitable branches were those with the happiest personnel; the employees and customers in those branches tended to remain with the company longer than those doing business with other parts of the bank. A rapid payoff in dollars and cents followed the company's shift to retain employees. Earnings per share rose from $0.70 to $1.10 in just three years, and customer retention increased to 95 percent compared to an industry norm of 88 percent. President Frank Schriner explained, "We learned that when our employees were delighted, they made our customers happy too."

For those who may question the value of work-life effectiveness in tough economic times, a survey of four hundred employers conducted by the Families and Work Institute in August 2009 found that 81 percent of employers have kept their existing work-life programs (reduced hours, phased retirement, compressed work weeks, telecommuting), and 94 percent of employers have added to their existing work-life programs, while 6 percent have eliminated their work-life arrangements. In the survey, employers with more than a thousand employees (16.5 percent of total employers) increased their work-life programs by 25 percent, and 37 percent have used flexible work-life arrangement to reduce layoffs. This occurred even though 66 percent of these employers report declining revenue over the past year and 64 percent of employers who have cut costs reduced their workforce.

Work-Life Programs and Policies

If an organization has a supportive and caring culture, it stands to reason that it would want to offer employees policies and programs that take care of personal and family needs that would otherwise hamper their ability to "be all they could be" at work. It is not only good public relations to be on lists such as the 100 Best Companies to Work For; it makes good business sense. There has been quite a bit of media attention paid to the work-life benefits some companies offer their employees. Some are truly perks, such as Google offering free bike repair and oil changes, or Calvert Funds awarding shoe subsidies for employees who walk to work. Some fit the purpose of the business, as with Honest Tea furnishing free drinks or the Club Managers Association of America giving free PGA tournament tickets. Many work-life programs and policies really help employees cope with myriad life issues, such as tuition assistance, onsite child care, eldercare counseling, rooms set aside for prayer and meditation, and a host of other options.

The Alliance for Work-Life Progress (www.awlp.org) is dedicated to advancing work-life as a business strategy, integrating work, family, and community. An entity of WorldatWork, AWLP defines and recognizes innovation and best practices, facilitates dialogue among various sectors, and promotes work-life thought leadership. It offers a self-audit on the website, which is reproduced in the accompanying box.

AWLP WORK-LIFE SELF-AUDIT
Overview
The Alliance for Work-Life Progress (AWLP) Work-Life Self-Audit will help assess the progress of your organization's work-life effort. After completing these steps, you will have:

- Evaluated your organization against the Categories of Work-Life Effectiveness
- Developed a strategy for aligning your work-life efforts with the core values of your organization

To begin:

1. Complete the self-audit.

   - Create an inventory of the work-life programs that fall into distinct categories.

   - Review your organization's strengths and weaknesses to determine the focus of any changes or modifications you may want to consider.

   Keep in mind that your company could have several strength areas.

2. Map a strategy for minimizing the gaps revealed in the self-audit.

   - This step provides a framework for setting goals to achieve new heights in your organization's work-life efforts in alignment with your organization's core values. The resulting "gap analysis" should be used to set goals for future work-life efforts in your workplace.

   Instructions: Check all programs, policies, and initiatives currently in place at your organization.

Caring for Dependents
Child Care:

- ☐ Onsite dependent care
- ☐ Dependent care travel-related expense reimbursement
- ☐ Child care resource and referral services
- ☐ Child care discount program with national providers

(Continued)

☐ Emergency backup child care service (organization-based or in-home care, school closing care)

☐ Special needs child care

☐ Child care subsidies

☐ After-school care programs

☐ Summer camps and activities

Other_____

Other_____

Parenting:

☐ Onsite caregiver support groups

☐ Onsite dependent care

☐ Workplace seminars and webinars

☐ Lactation support services (education, onsite mothers' room, lactation consulting)

☐ Support for grandparents raising grandchildren

Elder Care:

☐ Onsite dependent care

☐ Elder care resource and referral services

☐ Long-term care insurance

☐ Emergency backup elder care service

☐ Disabled adult care

☐ Geriatric counseling

☐ In-home assessments

Other_____

Other_____

Health and Wellness

☐ Employee assistance program

☐ 24-hour nurse line

☐ Fitness center facilities or affiliations

☐ Work-life seminars and webinars (stress reduction, financial planning, parenting, etc.)

☐ Weight management programs

☐ Smoking cessation assistance

☐ Onsite massages

☐ Stress management programs

☐ Voluntary immunization clinics

☐ Health screenings

☐ Nutritional counseling

☐ Onsite nurse

☐ Reproductive health and pregnancy programs

☐ Health advocate

☐ Occupational health programs

☐ Business travel health services

☐ Concierge service

☐ Workplace convenience services

Other_____

Other_____

Workplace Flexibility
Full-Time Options:

☐ Flex time

☐ Telecommuting

☐ Compressed workweek

☐ Alternative worksites

☐ Seasonal schedules

Other_____

Other_____

Part-Time Options:

☐ Part-time schedule

☐ Job sharing

(Continued)

☐ Phased return from leave

Other_____

Other_____

Financial Support

☐ Personal financial planning service

☐ Adoption reimbursement program

☐ Adoption assistance

☐ Tuition reimbursement program (student aid or loan programs)

☐ Dependent care flexible spending account

☐ College scholarships

☐ 529 plans

☐ Savings bonds

☐ Commuter benefits

☐ Voluntary benefits (i.e., auto, home, pet insurance, cancer, mortgage assistance)

☐ Pretax parking and transit benefits

☐ Accident insurance

☐ Legal plan

☐ Employee discounts

☐ Parking

☐ ID theft insurance

Other_____

Other_____

Paid and Unpaid Time Off

☐ Personal days and vacation

☐ Sabbaticals

☐ Paid holidays

☐ Paid family leave for new parents (fathers and domestic partners, as well as mothers)

☐ Short-term disability (STD)

☐ Long-term disability (LTD)

☐ General leaves of absence

Other_____

Other_____

Community Involvement
External Outreach:

☐ Community volunteer program

☐ Matching gift program

☐ In-kind donations

Other_____

Other_____

Internal Sharing:

☐ Shared leave program (donating personal or vacation time to others facing emergency situations, such as a child with terminal illness or other family catastrophe)

☐ Disaster relief fund

Other_____

Other_____

Culture Change Initiatives

☐ Diversity and inclusion initiatives

☐ Women's advancement initiatives

☐ Work redesign (efforts to reduce work overload and burnout)

☐ Team effectiveness

☐ Work environment initiatives

☐ Multigenerational issues

Other_____

Other_____

(Continued)

The alliance breaks down work-life *effectiveness* (which is becoming a more descriptive word than "programs and policies") into seven categories: caring for dependents, health and wellness, workplace flexibility, financial support, paid and unpaid time off, community involvement, and cultural change initiatives. They believe support for work-life effectiveness across organizations of all sizes and sectors has evolved over the past two decades, and these categories represent the range of programs and policies now in operation in all employment sectors. On the one hand, this list is not all-inclusive of the variety of benefits in the seven categories. On the other hand, the number of benefits is not as important as the quality and appropriateness of benefits in terms of the needs of the employees and the culture of the organization. What will really help employees manage personal needs such that they are less distracted at work? Given that the organization cannot meet every employee's needs, what are the employees' priorities in contrast to the organization's resources? Are there approaches that allow the most flexibility while maintaining efficient use of resources?

Another way to look at work-life effectiveness is to focus on issues. Flexible work arrangements and work-family conflicts are two of the more popular and most controversial issues facing both individuals and organizations.

Flexible Work Arrangements

There have been significant changes to families and lifestyles since the era of the father as sole breadwinner and the stay-at-home mom during the 1950s and 1960s. Dual-career couples, single working mothers, and the sandwich generation are just three among the many issues facing employers dealing with retention and productivity. Flexible work arrangements (FWAs) were developed to help employees cope with work-family pressures. Flex time was the first such arrangement, the concept that an employee can arrive at work within a two-to-three-hour window (say, 6:30 A.M. to 9:30 A.M.) and stay for eight hours. This allowed parents who needed to drop kids off at day care or school the needed time and still do a full workday. It also accommodated those people who wanted to get an early start and beat rush hour, or do errands. Early variations were the four-day, ten-hour-a-day work week, which allowed one day off a week; and the nine-day, nine-hours-a-day schedule that allowed one day off every two weeks.

Today it is common to see flex time, telecommuting, and compressed workweek arrangements in most organizations. Although many organizations offer these benefits, there are still issues as to which employees have access to them, whether employees who do have access take advantage of them, and how much control employees really have over their work schedule. Supervisors often have control over the administration of such policies, which might thus be applied unevenly and unfairly (Kelly & Moen, 2007). In addition, some FWAs have built-in rigidity, such as arrangements where you can telecommute only on certain days of the week; or flex time, where you have to be in the office during certain core hours; or compressed work schedules, where you can take off only Fridays. Last of all, some organizations offer these benefits but the unstated assumption is that if you take advantage of them too much or too often it could hurt your career advancement.

At the Seattle office of the U.S. Government Accountability Office, employees have to put in eighty hours every two weeks, but they can configure those hours however they choose except for one day a week for meetings. They can also telecommute some of the time (Sahadi, 2007). Kathy Bailey, founder of the Bailey Law group, let two employees work remotely after they moved away rather than lose them. One of the relocated employees brought in a new group of clients, tripling the company's revenue. Since 1991, employees who have been at American Express for ten years can apply for a paid sabbatical lasting between one and six months. The company asks that employees on leave work for a nonprofit or school of their choice.

Probably the most flexible plan is Best Buy HQ's ROWE program, or Results Only Work Environment (Kubal & Newman, 2008). Those organizational units covered by the ROWE program let employees work whenever and wherever they want as long as they get their work done. Since employees stopped counting the number of hours they work, they have been more productive. With the first experimental group of three hundred employees, turnover in the first three months of employment fell from 14 percent to 0 percent; job satisfaction rose 10 percent; and team performance scores rose 13 percent. The five-year-old plan now covers 60 percent of the employees at Best Buy's corporate headquarters. Employee productivity has increased an average of 35 percent in departments covered by the program.

Gap Outlet is only the second organization to have a ROWE program (Fox, 2009). It covers 137 headquarters employees and executives in merchandising, design, production, finance, HR, and IT. The company is very entrepreneurial, but it was burning out employees; 76 percent of the HQ staff are young women. The vice president of HR stated that the work is fun and challenging, but work-life balance was terrible and turnover was high. People in exit interviews would say that they love their job, but it wasn't worth it anymore. In February 2008, the Gap Outlet launched a ROWE pilot program within their production and technical services teams. The pilot produced significant results: production turnover dropped by 50 percent, and employee engagement scores improved 13 percentage points, the best in the division. As a result of the success of the pilot, Gap Outlet expanded it in September 2008 to include seventy-nine additional employees across the Gap Outlet and Banana Republic Factory Stores product and store support teams.

The fear with an experiment such as ROWE is that employees will never show up for work. Meetings will go unattended, calls will go unanswered, and deadlines will come and go without anyone there to notice. But ROWE is self-policing; employees ferret out those not doing the work because everyone is highly protective of the initiative. There is an unwritten agreement between the employees and the company that in exchange for the freedom to do their job in a way that makes sense for employees, they will perform highly. Gap leaders emphasize that the culture has to have a high degree of trust.

Work and Family Conflict

Gap Outlet was spending years investing in female leaders only to lose them after maternity leave because the women couldn't figure out how to swing both work and family. The company was losing a tremendous amount of experience and talent. Mothers with young children, especially single mothers, make up an increasing percentage of the workforce. In fact, the whole family picture in the United States is changing. It now includes an increasing number of single parents, same-sex partnerships, cohabiting couples, and biracial spouses, as well as blended, foster, and adoptive parent-child relationships. Such demographic realities have implications for workplace programs and practices (Johnson & Corday, 2009). The old norm of mom, dad, two kids, and a dog has changed. Families consisting of breadwinner dads and stay-at-home moms now account for just one-tenth of all households. Married couples with kids, who populated nearly every residence a century ago, now total just 25 percent—with the number projected to drop to 20 percent by 2010, according to the U.S. Census Bureau. Among married couples, with or without kids, dual-career households are now the most common type of household, representing approximately 40 percent of all working families. The transition from single-earner to dual-earner dominance changed the work-life balance dynamics of the workforce. Additionally, slightly more than half of married dual-career families have one child or more. But dual-career couples are not new. They have been around since the baby boomers started having families. What is new is that the U.S. Census Bureau's most recent figures show that married-couple households—the dominant cohort since the country's founding—have slipped from nearly 80 percent in the 1950s to just 50.7 percent today. This means that the nation's 86 million single adults could soon make up the new majority. Already, unmarrieds make up 42 percent of the workforce, 40 percent of home buyers, 35 percent of voters, and one of the most potent—if pluralistic—consumer groups on record.

According to Nicky Grist, executive director of the Alternatives to Marriage Project, "More of the workforce is going to be single, unmarried, or childless—or some combination. Employers need to recognize that marital status isn't a defining characteristic in the workplace any longer. It simply isn't a meaningful or reliable indicator of what's really going on in employees' lives" (Wells, 2007, p. 37). In fact, this demographic is fueling a backlash against family-friendly programs and policies, which have been the mainstay of work-life efforts in most U.S. (and European) organizations. Now what has been referred to as family-friendly is being changed to *employee-friendly*, with the focus on diversity and choice. One example is companies that bundle vacation, sick, and personal leave into one bank or pool of leave days that employees can use as they need. Some organizations offer cafeteria benefits, where employees get an amount of money or a percentage of their salary to allocate for a set of benefits according to their needs. Again, there are numerous varieties of work-life programs and policies that an organization can offer. What is most important is to meet employees' life needs in such a way as to acknowledge their whole selves. Jeff Chambers, vice president of human resources of the SAS Institute, has stated:

> SAS has a 30-plus year culture of deliberate inclusion and demonstrated regard for each and every one of our employees and their families. Our programs and policies are grounded in the basic, unassailable contention that *by actively anticipating, regarding and responding to the unique needs of employees and their families, we are directly impacting their ability to generate innovative ideas and products.* Whether an employee is a single parent of an adopted child, a grandparent raising his grandchild, a domestic partner, or a divorced boomer knee-deep in the sandwich of caring for a teen and a parent, we know they will feel better and do better when we show regard for their whole life, not just the skills they drive in the front gate every morning. It is simply good business. (Johnson & Corday, 2009)

Work-Life as an Integral Part of the Organizational Culture

Deloitte LLP was named to *Fortune* magazine's list of 100 Best Companies to Work for, for the tenth year in a row in January 2009. Like other companies, it has had several FWAs for employees, among other work-life benefits, for many years. But they found that FWAs did not seem to be addressing the career-life fit needs of employees. For one thing, FWAs were not integrated into the talent management cycle or processes. In addition, there was the perception that using FWAs implied an employee's lack of ambition and loyalty.

The Families and Work Institute found that 40 percent of working parents believe their job would be in jeopardy if they worked flexibly. In the legal profession, more than 20 percent of legal staff are interested in reduced work schedules, yet only 4 percent of lawyers take advantage of such programs.

Cathy Benko, vice chairman and chief talent officer for Deloitte LLP, and Anne Weisberg, a director in Deloitte's talent organization, tell this story to illustrate the limitations of FWAs:

> As a senior executive, Steve has had a traditional career in many respects. Always on the move, he scaled the corporate ladder as he built a series of successful business units within the same organization. His wife stayed home to raise their three children, returning to graduate school only when the kids were in middle and high school. In one respect, however, Steve is not so traditional. Ten years away from retirement, he wants to scale back his travel, even though this may limit his opportunities for leadership roles. "At this point in my life, my priorities are such that my faith and personal life come before the role I play within the organization," Steve explained. "I want to be true to my priorities." In other words, Steve wants options—options that have not historically existed for people at the top or on the fast track up the corporate ladder. In fact, for a variety of reasons including better health, financial gains, and personal preference, many baby boomers nearing retirement do not want to stop working completely, but they don't want to work in the same way they've been working either. What if an ingredient of the solution to the impending talent gap posed, in large part, by the retirement of the baby boomers was to offer options for customizing career paths such that employees could have their proverbial cake and eat it too? (Benko & Weisberg, 2009)

Benko and Weisberg developed a model of career progression and development called Mass Career Customization (MCC) that does just that. MCC is a framework for career progression and development that is based on the idea of a corporate lattice. In mathematics, a lattice allows one to move in many directions, is not limited to upward or downward progress, and can

Figure 6.1. The Four Dimensions of Mass Career Customization
Source: Benko, C., & Weisberg, A. (2009). Mass career customization. *Deloitte Review,* p. 58.
Retrieved March 6, 2009, from http://www.deloitte.com/view/en_US/us/Insights/Browse-by-
Content-Type/deloitte-review/article/35912ee3fad33210VgnVCM100000ba42f00aRCRD.htm.

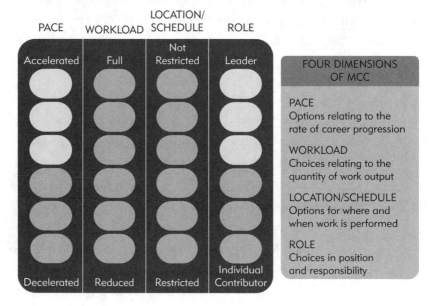

be repeated infinitely at any scale. In the real world, lattices are living plat-
forms for growth, with upward momentum visible along many paths. The
corporate lattice model allows multiple paths upward, taking into account
the changing needs of both the individual and the organization across various intervals of time. It can foster a new kind of loyalty, based on continuous
collaboration between employer and employee to design customized career
paths. The MCC framework is based on four sets of options, or four dimensions of a career: pace, workload, location and schedule, and role. The MCC
profile is a snapshot of each employee's career at a given point in time, and
it can be adjusted over time. Like adjusting the sound on a stereo equalizer
by moving the sliders up or down, MCC allows employees to dial up or dial
down to optimize their career path at varying life stages (Figure 6.1).

Although MCC offers options for multiple career paths, it does not open
the door to an infinite number of profile combinations. Deloitte's internal

results have shown that much of the time most employees will have a profile that looks more or less the same as the others. Even if they don't currently dial up or dial down, employees derive a *psychic benefit* from knowing that options and an organizational process for managing them are available should they need to deviate from normal, full-time employment status sometime in the future. There is also a cultural value that MCC serves by encouraging a framework for conversation between employee and employer regarding career choices. The transparency and shared responsibility for career planning that result from these structured conversations are critical components of a values-based culture.

Over time, every employee's MCC profile will exhibit its own path, recording the series of choices made over the course of the employee's career. For many, this path will look like a wave of sorts, with climbing and falling levels of contribution over time, as illustrated in the MCC Sine Wave in Figure 6.2. As this employee's career progressed, his level of contribution rose and fell. Although he is not fully dialed up today, he anticipates that state in the near future. As he explains, "I see a time in the not-too-distant future when I will want to dial up my career, in part so that my wife can dial down and spend time at home with the kids before they go off to college" (Benko & Weisberg, 2009, p. 56).

The Norm Is No Longer the Norm

Organizations concerned with issues such as talent recruitment and retention, sustainability, and living their values need to recognize that the traditional approaches for dealing with these issues are not going to work given the changes in the very nature of the workforce. Work-life programs and policies were developed to deal with typical baby boomer families. The growing prevalence of nontraditional families requires changes to existing workplace models of career development that were originally structured to match the traditional family model.

The number of women in the workforce is increasing. Today, nearly 60 percent of college graduates are women, and women hold more than half of all management jobs. As discussed in an earlier chapter, though, most women's lives do not fit the traditional career trajectory; in fact, many women have

Figure 6.2. The Mass Career Customization Sine Wave

Source: Benko, C., & Weisberg, A. (2009). Mass career customization. *Deloitte Review*, p. 59. Retrieved March 6, 2009, from www.deloitte.com/view/en_US/us/Insights/Browse-by-Content-Type/deloitte-review/article/35912ee3fad33210VgnVCM100000ba42f00aRCRD.htm.

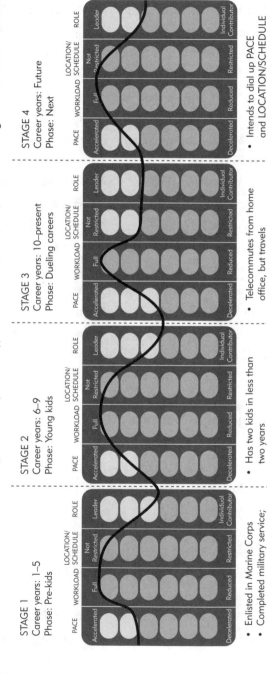

STAGE 1
Career years: 1–5
Phase: Pre-kids

- Enlisted in Marine Corps
- Completed military service; moved to manufacturing
- On accelerated career path
- Got married

STAGE 2
Career years: 6–9
Phase: Young kids

- Has two kids in less than two years
- Spouse scales back to 30-hour work week
- Rigid demands that he be available to work anytime, and be present at the plant whenever necessary, result in having to be "on call" all the time

STAGE 3
Career years: 10–present
Phase: Dueling careers

- Telecommutes from home office, but travels periodically for work; pace somewhat slower as a result

STAGE 4
Career years: Future
Phase: Next

- Intends to dial up PACE and LOCATION/SCHEDULE in the near future to allow his wife to dial down nonlinear or discontinuous careers. Some women are holding off on marriage and family while they get their career started, others are having (or adopting) children but staying single, and others are avoiding career commitment while they explore, learn experientially, and have fun.

Expectations on the part of men are also changing. More and more men have reached a point where preserving or increasing their personal time is more appealing than acquiring a bigger job and more money. A recent study found that 56 percent of senior executives surveyed would strongly consider refusing a promotion if it meant fewer hours available for their personal life. Men are participating more in family responsibilities, even if they are not yet on a par with women.

Both men and women of generations X and Y have high expectations for personal and work lives. They are technologically savvy, are adaptable to change, and are comfortable working nontraditional schedules and in non-office environments. Given advanced technologies, employers and employees can create new options for when, how, and where work gets done (Benko & Weisberg, 2009).

Much of this has been discussed previously in terms of individual job and career decisions. In Deloitte's case, it is a company that is responding to these same forces by creating a culture and a career framework that allows the flexibility and rewards people could find only by working outside an organization. Organizations need to adapt to the changing norms in much the same way individuals are, by developing a culture that values the needs of its employees.

7

Social Responsibility as Part of a Values-Based Culture

AS I STATED IN Chapter Five, meaningful workplaces recognize that social responsibility is an integral part of their organizational culture, not just good public relations. It is all about the alignment and interconnectedness of how an organization treats all its stakeholders and constituencies.

Corporate social responsibility (CSR) has evolved from early concerns about the impact manufacturing organizations have on the environment to a much broader concern for any organization's impact on employees, the surrounding community, society, and the planet. The World Business Council for Sustainable Development (WBCSD, 2000) defines CSR as the business commitment and contribution to the *quality of life of employees, their families* (italics added), and the local community and society overall. On the cover of WBCSD's annual report, the CEO of AT&T, C. Michael Armstrong, stated: "AT&T understands the need for a global alliance of business, society, and the environment. In the 21st century, the world won't tolerate businesses that don't take that partnership seriously, but it will eventually reward companies that do."

Despite the word *corporate* in the phrase, corporate social responsibility is not limited to profit-making entities. It is intended for any organization, whether professional or trade association, labor union, community-based organization, government agency (local, state, or federal), or other nonprofit (Lockwood, 2004). CSR, which is also referred to as corporate citizenship, is about accountability. Leaders are accountable not just to their employer but also to their employees. Employees are accountable to the organization, but they are also accountable to their communities. Organizations are not accountable just to their shareholders; they are also accountable to the society at large, to the global community, and to the planet. This is why Nike and Levi Strauss closed down "sweat shops" overseas and set strict humanitarian standards for foreign production, why the National Oceanic and Atmospheric Administration (NOAA) scientific and technical staff lend their expertise pro bono to help clean up the Chesapeake Bay, and why Starbucks buys a significant amount of fair-trade coffee and supports coffee growers who use sustainable agricultural practices. Meaningful workplaces understand that CSR is not only the ethical way to operate, but it's also good for business. An organization's image and reputation can be enhanced, and a number of studies have demonstrated that the financial performance of those companies known for their CSR actually outperform the companies in the S&P 500 Index as a whole. In a recent study, 82 percent of companies reported that CRS helps the bottom line and 74 percent said the public has the right to expect CSR (Lockwood, 2004).

Some organizations are going as far as referring to what is known as the "triple bottom line." Triple bottom line accounting attempts to describe the social and environmental impact that an organization's activities have, in a measurable way, on its economic performance, in order to show improvement or make evaluation more in-depth. John Elkington coined the phrase in his 1998 book *Cannibals with Forks: The Triple Bottom Line of 21st Century Business.* An example of such an attempt was Gap's 2004 social responsibility report, which was issued in response to concerns expressed about the clothing industry's use of sweatshops and child labor. Consider this statement from that report:

> In Cambodia, for example, we continue to support the International
> Labor Organization's (ILO) factory monitoring and training efforts,

which, according to a World Bank survey, are helping the country compete more effectively in the international apparel market. And we recently partnered with the International Finance Corporation's Mekong Private Sector Development Facility (IFC/MPDF) to launch a new managerial skills training program for factory supervisors. . . . (One owner's) factories (in India) provide workers with childcare facilities, free eye care and access to medical services. And he has incorporated sound environmental practices, like rainwater harvesting, into his operations. He sees that social responsibility is good business, and, as a result of his efforts, his turnover rates are low and his productivity is high. . . . Following the tsunami in South Asia, we reached out to support garment workers and their communities in the region. Gap Foundation double-matched employee contributions and donated additional funds to contribute $2.3 million to relief efforts. (p. 3)

The next step is for organizations to not only evaluate their responsibility to their own stakeholders but to also accept that they can play a role in alleviating social and environmental problems that go beyond their stated corporate mission, such as the Gap's tsunami relief efforts. Procter & Gamble won a CSR award for donating funds to help disadvantaged youths in Vietnam, combating child nutrition in India, and providing earthquake relief in Turkey.

If an organization is just starting to incorporate CSR into its culture, it is difficult to know where to start and how far to go. The Social Venture Network of business and social entrepreneurs is dedicated to the proposition that business can be a potent force for solving social problems. In 1995, they began to develop a set of standards for social responsibility at the urging of their members. Most of the leading thinkers and practitioners in the social responsibility arena were included among the more than 220 who contributed more than 650 individual criteria and hundreds of pages of insightful commentary. Both U.S. and European member organizations reviewed these criteria.

There are nine major categories in the SVN Standards (Goodell, 1999). Three are general topics—ethics, accountability, and governance—and six topics that are related to each organizational stakeholder: investors, employees, business partners, customers, community, and environment. The SVN

Standards begin with ethics because of the central role ethics play in corporate social responsibility: "Embracing this Principle requires a comprehensive, corporate-wide commitment to fundamental issues of honesty and human rights in dealings with all stakeholders. At its core, corporate social responsibility is an ethical choice, and the other Principles can be viewed as variations on this theme" (p. 4). Let's look at a selected list of some of the principles and practices that are particularly relevant for meaningful workplaces.

Principle: Employment Practices

The company engages in human resource management practices that promote personal and professional employee development, diversity at all levels, and empowerment. The company regards employees as valued partners in the business, respecting their right to fair labor practices, competitive wages and benefits, and a safe, harassment-free, family-friendly work environment. Here is a list of such practices.

- The company has written policies containing measurable objectives to promote diversity and empowerment in the work force. Performance against those measures is monitored and reported regularly to the board of directors and senior management.

- The company maximizes the participation of employees in corporate governance and enlists employees' help in improving the work environment.

- The company solicits employee advice in designing benefit plans that are flexible and portable. Benefits that can be used by low-wage workers are included, such as referral services, employee assistance plans, flex time, and tuition assistance.

- The company offers tuition reimbursement, internal training, and career development opportunities to all employees and encourages promotion from within the organization wherever possible. Mentoring relationships are encouraged.

- Training opportunities transcend the purely technical or professional to include life skills. The company attends to the financial well-being of employees with seminars on topics such as debt relief, retirement planning, tax assistance, elder care, and life management.

- The company takes a dynamic and integrated approach to addressing employees' economic, social, psychological, and spiritual needs.

- The company develops and communicates work-life policies and programs, such as flex time and day care, that support balanced work and personal lives.

- The company conducts regular employee and work-life surveys.

- The company monitors the employment practices of its suppliers, distributors, and business partners to encourage alignment with its own employment policies.

Principle: Community Involvement

The company fosters an open relationship with the community in which it operates, and the relationship is sensitive to the community's culture and needs. The company plays a proactive, cooperative, and where appropriate collaborative role in making the community a better place to live and conduct business. These are its practices:

- The company establishes formal mechanisms to maximize and promote two-way communication with the local communities in which it operates.

- Where appropriate, the company collaborates with community members to promote improvements in community health, education, workplace safety, diversity, and economic development.

- The company contributes to the local community through corporate policies and programs that explicitly encourage corporate charitable giving, employee volunteerism, and in-kind contributions of goods and services to local organizations.

- The company engages its employees and customers in choosing charitable causes.

- The company makes a special effort to train and employ marginalized, minority, and underemployed members of the local community.

The principle of employment practices identified three areas: employee development, empowerment, and diversity. The first several chapters discussed the critical need for learning and development, and empowerment, control, and self-efficacy. Development and empowerment are individual-based; diversity is group- and organization-based.

Diversity

One critical aspect of social responsibility is the responsibility to acknowledge and value the variety of diverse backgrounds that employees bring to an organization, and facilitate the synergy that can result from the mix of perspectives. As with much of what this book is about, there is a moral dimension to diversity, but there is a practical dimension as well. Nationally and globally, we are increasingly diverse societies. One can ignore this fact and cut oneself off from the benefits resulting from embracing a diverse workforce, or one can take advantage of what exists and will continue to increase.

According to a recent Society for Human Resource Management study, 86 percent of the organizations surveyed support diversity programs moderately to strongly. Moreover, diversity efforts are increasingly tied to specific business objectives. The study identified four main drivers of diversity in companies around the world:

1. Fairness and justice, ensuring an equal chance for members of disadvantaged groups

2. Guaranteeing a large enough talent pool in the future

3. Mirroring the customer base, increasing cultural competence, and delivering decisions that are based on a broader collection of considerations

4. Legal compliance

Although diversity is being increasingly embraced, for many organizations this means just hiring and counting the number of employees from different backgrounds. Yet, as David Thomas and Robin Ely (1996) point out in their *Harvard Business Review* article "Making Differences Matter," "When employees use their differences to shape new goals, processes, leadership approaches, and teams, they bring more of themselves to work. They feel more committed to their jobs—and their companies grow" (p. 3).

The diversity movement began as a way to ensure that people in minority groups were being treated fairly in terms of hiring and promotion. Inside the organization, the idea was to celebrate diversity by understanding and valuing differences among the workforce. Employee resource groups, support groups based on a specific difference (gender, race, sexual orientation, and so on), have become popular. These groups are a safe place to discuss issues related to diversity and also serve an educational function for the rest of the organization. They host brown bag discussions, hold social networking events, and sponsor human resource activities within the organization. In our research, we found that these groups have often identified specific needs of employees resulting in work-life initiatives. Unfortunately, what may start as a good intention by tapping into these groups for increased understanding about specific differences can backfire. Everybody in the group starts to be seen as representing just that group; their value is only in regard to their identity as a woman of color or as a gay Latino. Their value as a whole human being is ignored.

Now the focus has moved to *inclusion,* an organization culture that leverages diversity by building on people's strengths rather than their differences (Miller & Katz, 2002). Thomas and Ely (1996) talk about the assimilation paradigm and the differentiation paradigm. If an organization follows the former, then it really wants all employees to be the same. The organization believes that this is the only way to be fair to all employees, but it stifles divergent opinion, creativity, and challenges to assumptions. There is an interesting controversy about this paradigm, referred to as organizational fit. Strong organizational cultures require people to fit; otherwise you can have a lot of individual and group conflict and competition. But cultures that are too rigid and that require assimilation end up believing in one size fitting all. Numerous studies have shown that "lack of fit" is the most commonly faced challenge to nontraditional workers looking for jobs. The answer, also discussed elsewhere in this book, is to keep the values embedded in the culture constant, while supporting various means to achieve those values.

The other paradigm is the differentiation paradigm, which celebrates differences. This is often a means of matching differences to business needs. Latinos are asked to market to Latino communities; employees of color represent the organization at job fairs promoting inner-city hiring. Employees are put into boxes, and their full strengths are not used. They feel exploited and excluded.

Inclusion or integration values diversity by encouraging different perspectives to come together to deal with issues and solve problems. We know from small-group research that groups with diverse views and strengths generate more effective decisions than homogeneous groups. The key is that everyone buys into the goals and values of the group. But more important, people are allowed and trusted to be themselves, to be whole persons. This includes being able to inject all their experiences and learning into the organization.

Conclusion

Social responsibility has a strong moral dimension, and there are three levels of moral thinking that can be applied to the social responsibility of organizations.

1. *Preconventional morality.* The first, and most basic, level of moral orientation can be described as being based on what is in one's self-interest. In this case, the moral imperative is to do what is necessary to take care of oneself.

2. *Conventional morality.* If one's orientation is more focused toward those around one (those groups, networks, and communities that one identifies with), then one's moral orientation could be described at the second level and the moral imperatives will be to do what is best for the group.

3. *Transcendent morality.* The highest level of moral orientation would be if one is more committed to and focused on a higher consciousness or power. Here, the moral imperative will be in service to a higher calling.

At the lowest level are those organizations whose primary concerns are profits and shareholder value above all else. As long as one minimizes costs and maximizes the bottom line, then any means justifies the ends. The middle level is where most organizations reside; they will follow the norms of the industry. At the highest level are those that see social responsibility as a critical aspect of their organization culture.

Think about the implications of bottled water.

Thirty years ago bottled water hardly existed as a product; we drank water out of the tap in our kitchens, or out of a water fountain. In 2007 it was a $16 billion business (Fishman, 2007). Most of us don't think twice about paying money to buy a bottle of water that is (relatively) free. Most bottled water companies don't think about it either, yet one out of six people in the world does not have access to safe drinking water. In Fiji, a state-of-the-art factory spins out more than a million bottles a day of the most popular bottled water on the U.S. market, while more than half the people in Fiji do not have safe, reliable drinking water. Fishman noted that at the Peninsula hotel in Beverly Hills, where the rooms start at $500 a night, the minibar in all 196 rooms contains six bottles of Fiji water. The water in the Peninsula minibar is so desirable because of sales and the exposure with the Peninsula's clientele that the hotel gets a sales call a week from companies trying to dislodge Fiji.

Think about the fact that as of 2007, 24 percent of the bottled water we bought was tap water repackaged by Coke and Pepsi. Think about the fact that in excess of $1 billion worth of plastic water bottles, thirty-eight billion of them, are produced every year. In a world in which a billion people have no reliable source of drinking water, and three thousand children a day die from diseases caught from tainted water, what is the social responsibility of those organizations that bottle, sell, or supply bottled water for their clients and customers?

The moral implications of the products and services that organizations produce—whether for the employee who sweeps the floors at night, the CEO, the high school in the town, the citizens who watch their advertising on TV, or the fishermen on the river outside the plant—are what social responsibility is all about. Meaningful workplaces are, morally and ethically speaking, socially responsible workplaces.

8

Employee Engagement and Commitment

THE "SO WHAT?" QUESTION

THERE'S AN OLD JOKE about a CEO who is asked how many people work in his organization. His answer: "About half of them." According to the major consulting companies (Gallup, BlessingWhite, Watson Wyatt, and others) that have conducted research on engagement with their clients, about one-third of employees are fully engaged and about 20 percent are fully disengaged, with the rest somewhere between the two extremes. Although these companies, as well as academic researchers, all have slightly differing definitions of engagement, one that seems to cover all the others is that of the Conference Board: "A heightened emotional connection that an employee feels for his or her organization, that influences her or him to exert greater discretionary effort to his or her work" (Gibbons, 2006, p. 4).

Research published by Gallup and others has shown that engaged employees are more productive employees. The research also demonstrates that engaged employees are more customer-focused, exert greater effort, and are more likely to withstand temptations to leave. Many have assumed the connection between an employee's engagement and the level and quality of his or her performance. But this goes beyond performance, because engaged employees feel alignment among the mission of the organization, the organizational culture, their work, and their environment. Engaged employees are clear about what is expected of them, have the resources to complete their work, take advantage of opportunities for growth and feedback, and believe that they contribute significantly to the organization (Harter, Schmidt, & Hayes, 2002). Engagement is derived from work that challenges the employee without being psychologically or emotionally stressful and inspires a feeling of control over what happens at work (Emmott, 2006). As with the concept of flow, engaged employees find meaning and excitement in the work they perform. Disengaged employees, by contrast, are distanced from the rational and emotional components of work (Corporate Leadership Council, 2004); they may come to work physically, but they show no energy or passion in their performance. Disengaged employees focus more on their misery than on their work, usually spend all their time complaining, and distrust management and the organization (Shuck & Wollard, 2008). Disengaged employees cost the U.S. economy $250–300 billion a year in lost productivity, Rath and Clifton (2004) report; "When you add workplace injury, illness, turnover, absences, and fraud, the cost could surpass $1 trillion per year, or nearly 10 percent of the U.S. Gross Domestic Product (GDP)" (p. 1).

Watson Wyatt's 2008/2009 Work USA Report, "Driving Business Results Through Continuous Engagement," declared that engaged employees were twice as likely to be high performers as those who are less engaged (Hastings, 2009). They surveyed more than thirteen thousand full-time U.S. workers in May and June 2008. When employees are engaged, their organization enjoys higher productivity, has lower turnover, and is more likely to attract top talent. The companies whose employees reported being engaged earned 13 percent greater total returns to shareholders over the past five years than those who had a significant number of disengaged employees. Engaged employees missed 20 percent fewer days of work, and three-quarters of them exceeded or far exceeded expectations in their most recent performance review. They also found that engaged workers tended to be more supportive of organizational change initiatives and more resilient in dealing with change.

In the current economic downturn, with the scandal of bonuses being awarded to employees in companies that were given financial support from the federal government, it is important to note what Watson Wyatt reported: "During periods of turmoil—when the organization is undertaking cost-reduction measures, consolidations or other dramatic change events that will profoundly impact employees—maintaining or enhancing employee engagement can be critical to the organization's return to profitability" (p. 2). Those companies never grasped that it is not about the bonuses; it's about having meaningful work that engages you in an organization with a mission based on socially responsible sustainability rather than short-term profits. BlessingWhite found that 85 percent of employees who said they were engaged planned to stay with their organization (BlessingWhite, 2008). Younger workers have a new mind-set in that they expect employers to be more responsive to their work-life needs. They want the organization to deliver on its promises in a transparent, responsive, and mutually beneficial manner. Transparency involves open information sharing across all levels; responsiveness means listening actively to employees and taking timely action, and mutually beneficial means win-win solutions are sought.

To identify the elements of worker engagement, Gallup conducted hundreds of focus groups and many thousands of worker interviews in all kinds of organizations, at all levels, in most industries and in many countries. From these inquiries, researchers pinpointed, out of hundreds of variables, twelve key employee expectations that, if satisfied, constitute the foundation of strong feelings of engagement ("Gallup Publishes Long-Awaited Follow-up," 2006). The result was a twelve-question survey in which employees are asked to rate their response to each question on a scale of one to five.

1. Do you know what is expected of you at work?

2. Do you have the materials and equipment you need to do your work right?

3. At work, do you have the opportunity to do what you do best every day?

4. In the last seven days, have you received recognition or praise for doing good work?

5. Does your supervisor, or someone at work, seem to care about you as a person?

6. Is there someone at work who encourages your development?

7. At work, do your opinions seem to count?

8. Does the mission or purpose of your company make you feel your job is important?

9. Are your associates (fellow employees) committed to doing quality work?

10. Do you have a best friend at work?

11. In the last six months, has someone at work talked to you about your progress?

12. In the last year, have you had opportunities at work to learn and grow?

Another study of ten thousand employees in the UK found:

- Engagement declines as employees get older. But once they reach the oldest group of sixty plus, the level suddenly rises, showing this oldest group to be the most engaged of all.

- Minority ethnic respondents have higher engagement than their white colleagues.

- Managers and professionals tend to have higher engagement than their colleagues in supporting roles, although people in the latter group appear to owe greater loyalty to their profession than to the organization in which they practice their profession.

- Engagement declines as length of service increases.

- Having an accident or an injury at work, or experiencing harassment (particularly if the manager is the source of the harassment), has a big negative impact on engagement.

- Employees who have a personal development plan, and who have received a formal performance appraisal within the past year, have significantly higher engagement than those who have not (Robinson, Perryman, & Hayday, 2004).

This study concluded that the strongest driver of all was a sense of feeling valued and involved. This had several key components:

- Involvement in decision making
- The extent to which employees feel able to voice their ideas
- Managers who listen to their employees' views and value their contributions
- The opportunities employees have to develop their jobs
- The extent to which the organization is concerned for employees' health and well-being

The line manager clearly has an important role in fostering employees' sense of involvement and value. If employees feel involved and valued, their engagement and performance increase.

Employee Commitment

There seems to be a chicken-and-egg dilemma in the literature as to which came first, engagement or commitment. Scholars have been studying the psychology of commitment for a while and describe it as both a "willingness to persist in a course of action and reluctance to change plans, often owing to a sense of obligation to stay the course" (Vance, 2006, p. 4). Personal, work, and organizational commitment are portrayed in different ways. For example, people may go above and beyond to fulfill their work responsibilities as well as their family, personal, community, and spiritual obligations. Commitment can also emerge emotionally, in terms of people experiencing and expressing positive feelings about other people or events. Commitment has, further, a rational aspect in that most people consciously decide to thoughtfully plan and carry out the actions required to fulfill obligations. What seems to be one of the most important criteria for commitment is the level of congruence between the employees' values and work interests and the organization's values as manifested by the culture and opportunities for meaningful work

(Fornes, Rocco, & Wollard, 2008). The organization's culture is the principle driver of both commitment and engagement.

The model shown in Figure 8.1, by Jack Wiley, cofounder of Gantz Wiley Research (now part of Kenexa), shows how leadership practices, employee results based on those leadership practices, customer results of both leadership and work practices, and business performance are interrelated. The model is cyclical, showing that, over time, business performance also influences leadership practices.

Loyalty is used somewhat synonymously with commitment. Researchers surveyed nearly two thousand workers throughout the United States and found that the key drivers of employee loyalty include employee empowerment for decisions, trust between management and employees, opportunities for professional development, and active encouragement of creativity (Leonard, 2008). The researchers defined these attributes as key drivers of

---

Figure 8.1. Cyclical Implications of Leadership Practices

Source: Adapted from Wiley (1996).

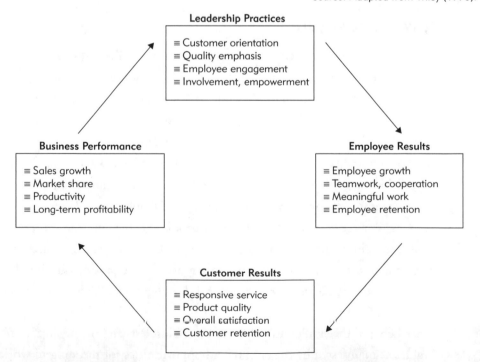

loyalty because the respondents ranked them as the most important factors and because other research has shown them to influence worker retention. Trust between employees and management is probably the most important factor, which ties in with other research concluding that the relationship between the employee and the immediate manager is one of the most critical factors in job satisfaction. The results of this study align with other research conducted on employee engagement and retention. All of the studies on employee satisfaction, engagement, commitment, and loyalty identify trust in immediate supervisors and senior management as a crucial element of the organization's culture. A recent study demonstrated that employees who trust their managers appear to have more pride in their organizations and are more likely to feel the organization is taking advantage of their strengths (Lockwood, 2007). The Corporate Leadership Council (2004) identified eight managerial characteristics that support commitment and engagement:

1. Managers are committed to diversity.
2. They take responsibility for both successes and failures.
3. They demonstrate honesty and integrity.
4. They help employees solve problems.
5. They respect and care about their employees.
6. They set realistic performance standards.
7. They model a passion for excellence.
8. They support their employees against adversity.

Trust in management is a value that has to be embedded in the culture of an organization; it cannot be practiced by just a few managers. The culture itself will be the primary driver of how engaged, committed, and loyal employees are.

According to Gamal Aziz, president of MGM Grand Hotel and Casino in 2001, Las Vegas was on a roll—and so was the MGM Grand (Byrnes, 2009). The five-thousand-room hotel was ringing up $175 million a year. The challenge for Aziz: to take something good and make it even better. Under his direction, revenue zoomed and the MGM Grand became the second most profitable hotel on the strip (after the Bellagio). Ask him what the single most important factor in this success was, and his answer is the employees. Now, with times getting tougher in Las Vegas as tourism drops and gambling revenues fall, he says his people have become even more critical to the company's success. "Employee engagement in times of difficulties and severe economic climate is far more profoundly important now," he says. "Employees are willing to give their all when they are well-treated, appreciated. And the ability to unlock that potential is a competitive distinction. It's their decisions, actions, and attitudes that really make the difference. Imagine taking ten thousand employees, and each and every one of them wanting to give more. That's really the difference between [us and] a company that has its employees just punching the clock and trying to get through the day." Aziz shares with employees the challenges he's facing. Employees, the CEO says, were what got the hotel to the next level, and they are the key to pulling through hard times. "We will get through this, we will survive," he says. "Once we get through this, the employees will be the ones who have gotten us through."

When Aziz arrived in 2001, he quickly sought out rank-and-file insight into the hotel and how it could improve. A survey of the hotel's ten thousand employees made clear that little information was being communicated to the staff about the events going on in the hotel daily, including such basics as who was staying there and what the hotel had to offer those particular guests. Employees sometimes didn't even know what convention groups were at the hotel. This made it difficult for staff to give a level of service that would affect customer loyalty, return visits, and spending in the hotel. Aziz came up with a simple fix. There is a short meeting now at the start of every shift in which every employee is given the rundown of what's happening in the hotel that day. Though a simple concept based on meetings that restaurants have long held to get waiters up on the daily specials, it's a major undertaking when rolled out across ten thousand employees every day.

All the investment in the staff, including extensive training and development, career development, and recognition dinners and other rewards, has led to more than 90 percent of MGM Grand employees saying they are satisfied with their job, and 89 percent saying their work has special meaning. "One of the ways we'll get through this dire economic circumstance we find ourselves in is if leaders set this tone that we're all in this together," Aziz reports. One consultant who has worked with a number of organizations on engagement issues considers the MGM Grand among the best at connecting with employees. Towers Perrin conducted a survey of tens of thousands of employees in six countries (including the United States, China, and India) and found that the primary action engaging employees is senior management's interest in their wellbeing.

Lest you think it is all well and good for large organizations, because they have the luxury of being able to afford all the training and benefits, you only have to look at programs such as Winning Workplaces' Top Small Company Workplaces and *HR* magazine's 50 Best Small and Medium Companies to Work for in America. The Winning Workplaces program is designed to identify and honor small businesses because they are often overlooked as examples of successful enterprises. To quote from the report of the 2008 competition:

> They make no secret of the fact that a key driver behind their success is their highly engaged and committed workforces. They work hard to intentionally select, prepare and retain their top talent and have built the kind of dynamic work cultures that maximize their talent. For all of these organizations, employees are critical to the success of the business, and that assumption is built into the business model. To sustain their competitive advantage and take on the "giants" in their industries, these small companies have wisely invested in developing their staff and intentionally built supportive and flexible workplaces. They actively involve employees in issues that affect the success of the business and their work lives. These companies have found a way to institutionalize and integrate many (employee-focused) practices so they become a part of the companies' culture and operation and enable them to thrive, even in difficult economic times. (Winning Workplaces, 2008. Copyright © Winning Workplaces. Reprinted with permission. www.winningworkplaces.org)

Going back to Jack Wiley's model depicted earlier, the process is cyclical. Values-based leadership encourages and supports employees who are engaged and committed to the organization, which is then rewarded and reinforced to continue to value its employees. All these elements are embedded in a values-based culture such that it is just "the way we do business here."

9

Reframing the Nature of the Workplace

CHARLES HANDY, the British management philosopher, echoed the work of Collins and Porras in *Built to Last* when he wrote that enlightened companies exist not just to make a profit but to achieve a "nobler end." The end is to produce an item or deliver a service that serves a need or a desire in society, and to do it in a way that is different or better than someone else. How organizations accomplish this is to bring together a group of people who can collectively do something that a single individual cannot. The organizations that are considered to be enlightened or progressive are the ones that see these people as *assets* to be valued and nourished, not just as economic *costs* to be controlled or eliminated.

The progress of humanism in the workplace (discussed in the first chapter) was a reaction to how workers were being treated. The reframing of the workplace at the time was about viewing workers as humans and not pieces of machinery that just needed a little oiling now and then. This paradigm more recently moved from how organizations treat people while they are working to responding to their family needs outside the workplace. The quality-of-work-life movement of the 1980s eventually gave way to the *work and family life* movement of the last fifteen years. The first issue that was acted on was women and their child care concerns. This broadened to encompass other family concerns and then personal needs. With programs such as the 100 Best Companies lists, the popularity of work-life programs and policies at organizations kept increasing. Employee satisfaction audits (such as Gallup's) were an impetus to identifying additional employee issues that could be met by human resource departments. Then organizations began to realize that supervisors needed to be trained to support the work-life programs so employees would feel comfortable taking advantage of them, and so managers would know how to use them for the mutual advantage of employee and organization. Finally, emphasis shifted from reducing work-life conflict by eliminating barriers to organizational effectiveness by increasing empowerment and engagement.

While work-life was gaining traction inside the organization, (corporate) social responsibility was increasing outside, and, as discussed in Chapter Seven, the philosophy of social responsibility started to encompass work-life as a broad-based humanistic mandate. In turn, this philosophy reshaped how the work itself was both structured and managed, and how the organization culture needed to be the foundation for all this change.

The Need to Reframe the Workplace

Virtual and self-directed teams, telecommuting "nomads," long-distance marriages, child care and elder care at the same time, and a host of other work and life differences from the traditional nine-to-five mental model are forcing the need to reframe the workplace. In addition, although academia has studied the workplace as a social system, it is only recently that the idea of *social capital* has been seen as something practically beneficial for organizations. Social capital refers to the connections among individuals, social networks and groupings, and the norms of reciprocity and trustworthiness that are the hallmarks of social cohesion. Organizations are social institutions by their very nature of being groups of individuals. Like small groups, which we know a lot about, the interaction within networks and groupings of people can yield enormous dividends or create enormous problems for organizations. The premise here is that if social capital is valued, it can contribute to the efficiency and effectiveness of organizations. Social capital furthers cooperation and collaboration because social relationships are built on trust and common goals are supported. In turn, these social relationships promote knowledge and resource sharing, which enhances individual growth and organizational learning. Social capital as part of the organization's culture reduces internal competitiveness, duplication of effort, low morale, and high turnover.

The workplace is the primary setting for social capital to flourish, although it plays a significant role in professional and trade associations, community groups, religious institutions, and others as well. As I have said before, most of us spend the majority of our day at work. The workplace relies on people working together and assisting one another. The workplace is a space in which employees build relationships that make the work more pleasurable. Actually, given that many people work long hours, have a long commute, and end up doing more work when they get home because of technology, their home lives and their family and friend relationships often suffer. So the workplace becomes the setting where they can form relationships that are supported by teamwork, having lunch together, traveling on business together, and spending time over the water cooler together. In addition, the workplace today is the most diverse social institution in our communities. The relationships started at work spill over into the community, which reinforces the workplace-community connection and the values of diversity and equality. Most important, the workplace can become a community unto itself—a workplace community.

Workplace Community

Ultimately, organizational culture is the primary vehicle for creating an environment of meaningfulness, engagement, and commitment. One environment that has held those values in societies was the *community environment*, where work, family, friends, and social life were intertwined. Tribes, villages, small towns, and tight-knit neighborhoods have all demonstrated the value of community. The workplace as community can and does exhibit these same values.

Community can be defined as a body of individuals organized into a group with awareness of some unifying values and purpose. Community requires the presence of interdependent connections and shared ideas among its members. In neighborhoods, towns, and villages, how people relate to one another and contribute to the betterment of the community can make the difference between a great place to live and a bedroom community where people just come home to eat and sleep. In great places to work, employees feel a part of a work community where everyone is working toward a common mission and relationships between employees and managers, as well as among employees (such as those in work teams), are supportive and nurturing. Cooperation and collaboration are valued more than internal competition and conflict. Friendship and fun are more valued than status and workaholism. The majority of employees are engaged and committed rather than apathetic and cynical. French and Bell (1998) identified a number of characteristics (among others) that should be present in work communities:

- Employees feel included and work hard to include others (new employees, customers, suppliers, other stakeholders)
- Employees like what they are doing and like each other
- Employees participate in setting goals, solving problems, and strategic planning
- The organization values individuality, creativity, and diversity
- There is a strong sense of high performance and excellent service
- Employees feel fairly rewarded and recognized
- The organization values ethical behavior and personal integrity
- Everyone feels responsibility for leadership behaviors and for group effectiveness
- Employees work hard and play hard
- Everyone shares a sense of purpose about the mission of the organization and how one's work fits into that purpose.

French and Bell, whose work on organization development is one of the more popular books in the field, predicted in their sixth edition that the search for community in the workplace would be a priority for both OD practitioners and organization leaders as we move into the twenty-first century.

Jeff and Barbara Black own four restaurants in the Washington, D.C., metropolitan area. None of their executive chefs are celebrities or studied under famous chefs in premier restaurants, but at least three of the four restaurants are on the 100 Best Restaurants list of the *Washingtonian* magazine every year. Chefs are often notorious for being autocratic and controlling; Jeff believes that if you give up control, offer guidance and expectations, and let people think for themselves, you get better results than trying to micromanage. The executive chefs at his restaurants have moved up from the lower levels in the kitchen. In one restaurant, the current executive chef started out as a customer who expressed an interest in cooking and was offered an entry-level job. Jeff believes anyone can contribute, so all are given a chance. Instead of the kitchen staff eating leftovers, the junior staff cooks for everyone so they can improve their skills and get feedback. Midlevel cooks can go into the refrigerator in the morning, look at what's available, and create dishes on the spot. What they create in the morning could be the special for the evening. Jeff believes everyone has strengths and can contribute to the whole experience. When he decided to open an upscale seafood restaurant with a fish market, he realized he needed a fishmonger. Instead of hiring one from the outside, he tapped one of his kitchen staff and said that he would provide the resources for this person to become a knowledgeable and skilled fishmonger. Without any prior experience, this staff member is now considered to be one of the Washington area's experts on fish—all because Jeff believed he had the potential and instilled that belief ("You train them, trust them, and then let them go").

Everyone pitches in at his restaurants. If Jeff shows up at one of his establishments during a snowstorm and everyone is busy inside, he will pick up a shovel and clean the sidewalk. Work schedules are set every two weeks, but if someone is sick or needs a day off for an unplanned situation, someone else will always jump in. In the kitchen, the work is hard, with all but the upper-level chefs paid by the hour and not getting benefits (which is standard in the restaurant industry); but the staff feel that their being treated with respect and trust, and feeling like a group, outweighs any perks they might get at other kitchens (such as at hotels). So when an upper-level chef who is a single mom needed help with child care, management worked out a flexible schedule and her fellow staff members helped out with her responsibilities. Suppliers are treated the same way. During the inauguration of President Obama, with millions of people coming into the metropolitan area, restaurants (among other businesses) were warned about street closures and transportation disruptions for days before and during the event. Jeff's suppliers made sure he received his deliveries well before the streets and bridges were blockaded; other restaurants didn't fare as well.

Staff often socialize together, and Jeff and Barbara have staff parties, outings, and ball games throughout the year. Cooks will travel together to other cities to sample restaurant cooking. Everyone has the potential to move up in the business. An executive chef wanted experience in the dining room, so he was given the opportunity to move over and eventually was appointed the general manager of the restaurant. He now works in the corporate office. His move, in turn, allowed his assistant to move up to the executive chef position. Jeff even finds satisfaction in an unlikely way: "Success is having employees leave for a better position" at another restaurant.

Jeff, Barbara, and the rest of the leadership of the Black Restaurant Group have built a work community. One chef at a rival restaurant described the environment as true group synergy, with every staff member feeding off the others. You can see the pride, the commitment, and the camaraderie that exists in each workplace. The leadership sets the culture, the culture sets the community environment, employees thrive, customers are satisfied, suppliers and vendors want to work with the organization, and all this positive feedback reinforces the leadership to keep doing what they are doing. John Gardner, the well known presidential advisor, educational reformer, activist, author, and philosopher, wrote a piece in 1989 on moral leadership. He discussed the virtue of a morally healthy society that produces communities (including the workplace) that impart coherent value systems. In a dysfunctional value system, people lose their sense of meaning and feel powerless. They doubt they can influence the life of the community. They yearn for individual responsibility and commitment. In other words, they become *disengaged* The values-based culture of workplace community incorporates the characteristics that drive engagement and commitment.

Wile (2001) and Small (2009) conducted two of only a handful of research studies on work communities. Wile interviewed representatives of ten for-profit organizations that were known for their commitment to community building and then built a model and submitted it to a panel of OD consultants. He found that three major themes emerged: leadership, values, and structure. Leadership was focused on what he called the double bottom line of people and profits. Leadership also needs to be committed to people-centered values, adequate resources, and a long-term perspective. The values he identified as being paramount for workplace community building were respect, trust, inclusion, and celebration. Structure was about honoring people, allowing maximum communication, promoting employee owner-ship, holding people accountable, and seeking collaboration. One statement repeated in various ways was that if the organization took care of its people the people would take care of the organization. In every organization, the culture instilled a sense of community and generated commitment among the employees. The workplace community was a place that created belong-ing, trust, caring, and a reason for sharing and celebrations. Small con-ducted a case study of one government agency and found substantially the same findings as Wile but in addition identified personal relationships and connections as being critical to the workplace community. Small also reported that how the workspace was designed helped facilitate a sense of community and support relationship building. Comfortable lounge spaces for informal communications and an adjacent kitchen for snacks and drinks, picnic tables outside where employees can have lunch together on nice days, and paths through wooded or landscaped areas for walks all support relation-ship building.

Actually, one consulting company, the Work Design Collaborative, has identified several design principles for meaningful workplaces:

- Include social spaces in the building. They support relationship and team building, as well as the creativity and divergent thinking that emerge from informal workspaces.

- Make the workspace flexible. Everyone is different, so the more employees can create their own unique workspace, the more in control they will feel. The more comfortable employees are, the more productive they will be.

- Think of the work facility as you would a residence, with rooms for different needs. Most organizations have meeting rooms that are used for everything other than individual work. Some organizations have rooms for meditating, comfortable rooms for teams to brainstorm, and even rooms for power naps.

Some organizations use artwork in the halls for inspiration and reflection and some have "playrooms" with games. The important point the Work Design Collaborative makes is to pay attention to how employees use space, ask them what they would prefer, and watch how they tend to come together and for what purpose. The more flexible the workspaces, the more easily they can be adapted for changing needs.

A different kind of work community has sprung up for virtual workers. It started at neighborhood coffee houses, where people would gather with their laptops because they didn't want to work alone at home. People would connect, agreeing to come at the same time on certain days, and out of this arrangement emerged virtual work communities. Then someone got the idea of creating a community office space for virtual and teleworkers. For a daily or monthly fee, you get a desk, use of office equipment, a kitchen, meeting space, and a lounge. Your social needs are also met through informal interactions and more formal networking events, holiday parties, and the like. This may not be a work community in an organizational sense, but it is affording community through social and networking interaction. In some instances, this co-working arrangement has led to business incubation that can result in community being a foundational part of the culture from the start.

SAS: A Workplace Community with a Values-Based Culture

SAS was called the most important software company you never heard of by *Fast Company* magazine in 1999. Even today, though many MBA students, corporate work-life directors, and HR professionals are familiar with their background, they are not a household name. They started as a statistical analysis software company (hence the initials "SAS") based near Raleigh, North Carolina, and since 1976 they have been a company where engagement and commitment matter more than salary, stock options, and bonuses.

The SAS philosophy, as stated on their website, is simple:

"If you treat employees as if they make a difference to the company, they will make a difference to the company."

That's been the employee-focused philosophy behind SAS's corporate culture since the company's founding in 1976. At the heart of this unique business model is a simple idea: satisfied employees create satisfied customers.

SAS employees work in an environment that fosters and encourages the integration of the company's business objectives with their personal needs. With enviable low employee turnover that has been consistently and significantly below the industry average, SAS reaps the rewards of employee loyalty and the benefit of the most talented minds in the software business. (www.sas.com)

SAS has an amazing array of benefits, from an onsite fitness center, child care center, and swimming pool to dry cleaning, massage, health care, and skin care services. Employee benefits are extensive, but they are also of very high quality. The child care center is not just a babysitting service but is staffed with fully trained Montessori professionals. The health care center staff has been trained by the Brazelton Institute in Boston.

There are no limits to the number of sick days an employee can take, even to care for family members. "We've worked hard to create a corporate culture that is based on trust between our employees and the company," explains SAS President and CEO Jim Goodnight, "a culture that rewards innovation, encourages employees to try new things and yet doesn't penalize them for taking chances, and a culture that cares about employees' personal and professional growth" (SAS website). They offer flexed and compressed work weeks, but they don't track employee usage. In other words, employees are trusted to get their work done without having to account for time worked.

Time off is given to meet with an aging parent's hospice care provider or a child's teacher. The environment is open and collegial, and employees and managers could be found mingling informally in one of their many open spaces, or playing a pickup game of basketball, at any time of day. There is no dress code, and every employee has his or her own office and can take advantage of an in-house ergonomics consultant to help with picking out furniture. Open and honest communication is highly encouraged, and there is an extensive intranet system. As one report states, dealing with what are perhaps minor or extraneous issues (such as suggestions for a day off for the opening of a new movie, or for changing the toilet dispensers in the bathroom) are a small price to pay weighed against an environment populated by open and informed employees.

It goes without saying that they put the same effort into their community involvement and philanthropic giving as they do toward their employees and customers. Employees have volunteered thousands of hours a year; the company donates used computers and office furniture to schools, funded a community learning center at a public housing community, and created an online database with profiles of all the participants at the 2003 international Special Olympics.

The SAS business model is aligned with how employees are treated. Every product that goes out the door has the names of all the employees who worked on the project. As a result, employees truly own their team's accomplishments. Customers often call the individual software engineers for advice and support, and they are encouraged to do so. SAS software is licensed to customers annually, and customers don't have to renew their contracts. To keep customers as long-term partners, the company must supply them with excellent service and constant upgrades. Customers typically work hand in hand with SAS employees to improve products. Customer turnover is even lower than employee turnover.

Finally, professional and career development is highly supported and encouraged. Over the years, employees have moved from administrative positions to regional sales management, from food service attendant to corporate event planner. The company has never laid off an employee in its more than thirty years, and annual turnover has never exceeded 5 percent. The SAS philosophy on employee performance is predicated on intrinsic motivation and trust. Basically, SAS makes sure employees have the resources they need to get their job done, and then the company gets out of the way. Employees are encouraged to do research and to "work on the edges."

SAS's values and beliefs, as embodied in their culture, clearly were the foundation for an engaged and committed workforce. Research has demonstrated that organizations with cultures like the SAS culture, which have meaningfulness, supportive managers and co-workers, and available resources, are more likely to have engaged employees (Lockwood, 2007). Because of their reputation and the networking of their employees, they also attract and retain the best talent.

Conclusion: Reframing Back to the Community

The prevailing paradigm of organization structure has been the image of a machine (Morgan, 1996). Order, control, authority, discipline, rigid job descriptions, and multiple layers of leadership are just some of the features of the bureaucratic model of organizational functioning. Communities, by contrast, are founded on a more natural way of functioning in the world. People come together to serve a mutual purpose and they work, play, and celebrate together in self-governing, interdependent relationships. Reframing the workplace on the basis of a more humanistic, natural structure calls for a profound philosophical shift. If work is part of the human condition, the workplace should mirror a more natural, human way of working. The workplace community fosters creativity, innovativeness, divergent thinking, excitement, sharing, social responsibility, challenge, learning, and meaning. The work community culture philosophically values authenticity, shared decision making, caring for others, and engagement and commitment to a common mission and vision. The work community as a meaningful workplace also makes good business sense, because in the short run it reduces turnover and eliminates low morale, and in the long run it promotes sustainability.

10

Integrated Wholeness at the Individual and Organizational Levels

AS NOTED IN CHAPTER ONE, one of Maslow's earliest works described the key principles he believed must be included in any theory of human motivation. He believed that "the *integrated wholeness* of the organism must be one of the foundation stones of motivation theory" (Maslow, 1943, p. 370; emphasis added).

People strive to become whole, or to complete themselves, through their choices and activities, including their work. A new discontent and restlessness will soon develop, unless the individual is doing what he is fitted for. A musician must make music, an artist must paint, a poet must write, if he is to be ultimately happy. What a man *can* be, he *must* be. This need we may call self-actualization. . . . It refers to the desire for self-fulfillment, namely, to the tendency for him to become actualized in what he is potentially. This tendency might be phrased as the desire to become more and more what one is, to become everything that one is capable of becoming. (p. 377)

Both individuals and organizations strive to be more; the big question is, More of what? Dian Svendsen (1997) conducted a heuristic study of six women (including herself) and how they integrated their work and the rest of their lives. She found the "more" related to the quality of their lives. As the women put more of themselves into their work, their whole lives in turn were enriched, which allowed them to further enhance their work. It was a growth spiral that led to higher fulfillment and self-esteem, rich relationships with others, increasing connectedness to one's purpose and values, and even a more significant sense of spiritualness. Organizations can also move through a growth spiral in which the more employees feel engaged and supported, the more they feel committed to the organization; the more they feel committed, the more the organization offers meaningful work and growth experiences and supports the whole employee. The organization prospers in the good times, survives through the bad times, and is sustainable. For both the individual and the organization, it's a win-win situation.

Integrated Wholeness at the Individual Level

I ended the last chapter by discussing the organization as a work community, and the feeling of interconnectedness that such an environment creates. In Chapter One, I identified the sense of disconnectedness that many people feel in their work, which is similar to the phenomenon of disengagement. At the individual level, the focus is on feeling disconnected or disengaged from the work one performs. Does it fit your values and purpose? Does it fit the environment in which you would like to work? Does it fit the current stage of development of your life? *Does it fit who you are?* Whether a job fits or not is like trying on a piece of clothing; you know when it fits just right in terms of look and feel. Most of us will know it if our work fits in the same way. Fit is about who we are, what we want to do, and who we want to do it with. Fit also has to do with the whole person. Mentally and spiritually, is the work personally fulfilling? Am I helping others? Am I making a contribution to society? *Is this what I am meant to do?* Emotionally, do I enjoy the work? Is it fun? Do I look forward to it on most days? Psychologically, does it fit my lifestyle, my stage in life, what I want (or need) to be doing at this point in my life? Am I learning, developing, growing in terms of knowledge, skills, and abilities? Does what I do matter—make a difference for me and for others in my life and in society as a whole?

Remember that there is no prescription for finding what fits. Books and job counselors will tell you that if you just follow their ten easy steps, you will find your passion. But the research, and most people's experience, says that it doesn't work that way. You have to know yourself first, and the more you know about yourself, the clearer you will be about what you are looking for. Then you have to be open to opportunities, and not limit yourself to jobs that don't pay what you think you ought to earn, or don't have the status you would like to achieve, or don't have the title with which you can identify. There is one danger to being clear about your passion: that you might become too rigid about what fits your passion. This is why I suggest being open to opportunities. Not that you should settle for second best, but you don't know what all the possible kinds of work are out there that would meet your purpose.

Learning, challenge, creativity, personal growth, self-actualization, personal mastery . . . throughout the first half of this book, I kept cycling back to learning. Learning is such a powerful force because it gives you the tools, the resources, the plans, and the material to be what you want to be. As I mentioned in Chapter Three, people with meaningful work see learning as fuel and their work as a journey. It's not about the destination; it's about the day-to-day ride. You want to have the best high-octane fuel you can get for the ride. Being on the journey means not only having the resources but also being able to plan your own trip. So having autonomy and control allows you to be the driver. Having self-confidence allows you to steer safely around obstacles. Believing in personal mastery and self-actualization means being the best driver you can be. I know this all sounds like something a motivational speaker would say, but those who see themselves as master of their own destiny more often continue to reach beyond their achievements than those who feel they have little or no influence on their own lives.

How we spend our nonworking life says as much about us as our work identity. The *quality* of the time we spend being parents, family members, friends, volunteers, neighbors, and ourselves is important to our overall physical, mental, and emotional well-being. Our overall well-being affects our performance at work, which is why it is so important to manage the tensions between work and the rest of life. We all struggle with our time, and wish we had more of it. We all have the same twenty-four hours in a day, and when we reach the age that the baby boomers are now at we don't want to look back and regret not spending more time with the kids, not going away more with our spouse or partner, not seeing our friends more, and not taking care of ourselves. By then it is too late. Think out and plan out your career goals and your life goals while you are young, and then be prepared to alter them as needed.

Integrated Wholeness at the Organizational Level

We are all stakeholders in numerous organizations, whether as employee, vendor, investor in a mutual fund or a pension fund, board member, or customer. If we are treated as a stakeholder, we are likely to want to remain a stakeholder. If we are treated as a "necessary evil," then we are likely to go elsewhere. As employees, even in economically hard times, we have choices. There are still job openings; there are still entrepreneurial opportunities, if not today, then tomorrow. If we stay at our present organization but are dissatisfied and disengaged, of how much value are we to the organization? Supposedly, the best and brightest left the organizations that were hardest hit by the economic downturn because they didn't want to be associated with a sinking ship. My guess is that the financial institutions that were more ethically responsible and focused on sustainability rather than profits did not lose as many professionals as others. It seems that when organizations concern themselves with short-term ends (profits and *share*holder values) rather than the means to the ends and to longer-term ends, they often get into trouble. Organizations looking for a quick fix often try to implement the latest management approach, and then when it doesn't work they blame the approach. Organizations that are committed to the long run may implement the same approach but embed it in day-to-day operations such that it becomes part of the culture. Organizations that have values-based cultures see a moral imperative for treating all stakeholders with respect, trust, and integrity. Organizations reap what they sow; "toxic" companies drive people away. There isn't a scarcity of good talent or loyalty, but there is growing unwillingness to work for toxic organizations. Jeffery Pfeffer at Stanford University disagrees that people are not interested in long-term careers anymore. "I don't believe that people are looking to go flitting from one job to the next," he says. "People are looking for the opportunity to have variety in their work and to tackle challenging assignments. The best companies are figuring out how their employees can have both opportunities—without leaving" (Webber, 1998b).

Pfeffer goes on to say that all that separates a company from its competitors are the skills, knowledge, commitment, and abilities of the employees: "There is a very compelling business case for this idea: Companies that manage people right will outperform companies that don't by 30% to 40%. . . . Studies of the steel industry, the oil-refining industry, the apparel industry, and the semiconductor industry all demonstrate the enormous productivity benefits that come with implementing high-performance, high-involvement management practices. There is conclusive evidence that holds for all industries, regardless of their type, size, or age. The results are the same."

Values-based leadership is based on a simple premise: lead the way you would like to be led. Most people would rather be guided and supported than pushed and micromanaged. Most people would like to be trusted to do a good job, and to have the resources to grow and excel. Values-based leadership takes less energy and time than other styles of leadership, because it shifts responsibility and ownership to the employee. Engaged and committed employees do not need heavy leadership. They are aligned with the values and mission of the organization; they care about their work and want to go the extra mile for their colleagues, their leaders, and the organization. Engaged employees often have a good working relationship with their managers; values-based leaders often have a good working relationship with their employees. It is a win-win situation.

Values-based cultures view the surrounding community, the nation, the global community, and the planet as extensions of their responsibility to their employees. If their employees are engaged, their people are also usually engaged in the communities in which they live. Just as the individual needs to balance work and the rest of life, the organization needs to balance its mission to produce a product or service with responsibility to the rest of society. The quality of the product or service, how customers are treated, and the ripple effect of that product or service through the larger society need to be in alignment. REI, the outdoor clothing and equipment company, treats its employees, customers, and the mountains, trails, and rivers on which customers use their products with equal respect. Starbucks treats employees, customers, and coffee growers with equal respect. *It all fits together.*

Building the Meaningful Workplace

It's not about the perks; it's about the culture. Employees of meaningful workplaces are not there just because they have great benefits. The benefits are a result of the values-based culture. The culture has to be embedded with values of trust, respect, fairness, challenge, growth, caring, and social responsibility, or else it's just window dressing and employees will see through it.

The organization supports the whole person and the whole person is engaged in the organization. Although no organization can be all things to all people, meaningful workplaces strive to recognize and support employees' work, family, leisure, personal, and community needs. In turn, employees will be engaged and committed because they have meaningful work and their work is aligned with their individual purpose and the organization's mission and values. This is integrated wholeness at the organizational level.

The organization is truly a community. When you go to work every day knowing that what you do makes a difference, that your voice is heard, that your work is meaningful, and that you enjoy the company of your colleagues and managers, then you are truly part of a workplace community. You feel ownership of the mission because you are proud to be associated with the organization. When people know they are applying their efforts and talents to the purpose of a group, they truly feel it is their community; "artificial" motivators become superfluous. Meaningful workplaces are synergistic. The employees feed off the organization and the organization feeds off its employees. It goes right back to the interconnectedness that existed when where you lived, where you worked, and with whom you socialized were one and the same.

Neal Chalofsky is a professor and director of the Human and Organizational Learning (formally the HRD) Graduate Program at the George Washington University, Washington, D.C. He is also president of Chalofsky Associates, an OD/HRD consulting firm.

Previously he was a professor and director of HRD graduate studies at Virginia Tech. He has also been an internal OD/HRD practitioner, manager, and researcher for several federal government and corporate organizations.

Chalofsky has consulted with such organizations as the Organization of American States, Mobil Research & Development Corporation, U.S. Department of Education, Computer Sciences Corporation, U.S. Chamber of Commerce, the Smithsonian Institution, Ernst & Young, the World Bank, the National Alliance of Business, and Verizon (then Bell Atlantic). He has also worked with the Postal Service in South Africa, ICI International in Taiwan, and Grupo Alpha in Mexico.

He has been a member of the national board of directors and chair of several national committees of the American Society for Training and Development, as well as past president of the Washington, D.C., chapter. He is also a founding member of the Academy for Human Resource Development. He has been a speaker at numerous national conferences, such as the American Society for Training and Development, the Association on Employment Practices and Principles, and the Organization Development Network. He was a keynote speaker at the first annual conference of the New Zealand Society for Training and Development and has also presented at conferences and meetings in Singapore, Taiwan, Australia, Ireland, and South Africa.

He is a research fellow of the Center for the Study of Learning at GWU. He is also a member of the editorial board of the *Human Resource Development Quarterly* and is a reviewer for *Human Resource Development Review* and *Human Resource Development International.*

Chalofsky is coauthor of *Effective Human Resource Development* and *Up the HRD Ladder* as well as the author of numerous chapters of edited works and journal articles.

REFERENCES

Ackoff, R. L. (1981). *Creating the corporate future: Plan or be planned for.* New York: Wiley.

Alderfer, C. P. (1972). *Existence, relatedness and growth: Human needs in organizational settings.* New York: Free Press.

Anderson, S., Cavanaugh, J., Collins, C., Pizzigatti, S., & Lapham, M. (2008). *Executive excess 2008: How average taxpayers subsidize runaway pay.* Washington, DC: Institute for Policy Studies, and Boston, United for a Fair Economy.

Anderson, T. (1991). *Making sense of the sixties* [Booklet accompanying video series of same name.] Washington, DC: PBS Video.

Argyris, C., & Schön, D. (1974). *Theory in practice: Increasing professional effectiveness.* San Francisco: Jossey-Bass.

Axelrod, R. (2000). *A brief history of motivation.* Unpublished manuscript, George Washington University, Washington, DC.

Bandura, A. (1986). *Social foundations of thought and action: A social cognitive theory.* Englewood Cliffs, NJ: Prentice Hall.

Bandura, A. (1997). *Self-efficacy: The exercise of control.* New York: Freeman.

Beazley, H. (1997). *Meaning and measurement of spirituality in organizational settings: Development of a spirituality assessment scale.* Unpublished doctoral dissertation, George Washington University, Washington, DC.

Benko, C., & Weisberg, A. (2009). Mass career customization: Building the corporate lattice. *Deloitte Review.* Retrieved March 6, 2009, from http://www.deloitte.com/view/en_US/us/Insights/Browse-by-Content-Type/deloitte-review/article/35912ee3fad33210VgnVCM100000ba42f00aRCRD.htm

BlessingWhite. (2008). *The state of employee engagement, 2008: North American overview.* Retrieved March 22, 2009, from www.blessingwhite.com/research

Block, P. (1993). *Stewardship: Choosing service over self-interest.* San Francisco: Berrett-Koehler.

Briskin, A. (1996). *The stirring of soul in the workplace.* San Francisco: Jossey-Bass.

Bronson, P. (2002). What should I do with my life? *Fast Company, 66,* 69–75.

Burns, J. (1978). *Leadership.* New York: Harper & Row.

Byrnes, N. (2009, January 16). *The issue: Maintaining employee engagement.* Retrieved September 7, 2009, from www.businessweek.com/managing/content/jan2009/ca20090116_444132.htm

Cameron, K. S., & Quinn, R. E. (2006). *Diagnosing and changing organizational culture: Based on the competing values framework.* San Francisco: Jossey-Bass.

Catalyst. (2001). *The next generation: Today's professionals, tomorrow's leaders.* New York: Author.

Chalofsky, N. (1996). A new paradigm for learning in organizations. *Human Resource Development Quarterly, 7,* 287–293.

Chang, E. (2008, February 10). Making it: Auto body repairman finds fulfillment in steering own career. *Washington Post Sunday Magazine.* Retrieved March 20, 2009, from www.washingtonpost.com/wp-srv/artsandliving/magazine/making-it/021008.html

Collins, J., & Porras, J. (1994). *Built to last: Successful habits of visionary companies.* New York: HarperCollins.

Corporate Leadership Council. (2004). *Driving performance and retention through employee engagement.* Washington, DC: Author.

Crawford, M. (2009). *Shop class as soulcraft: An inquiry into the value of work.* New York: Penguin Press.

Crittenden, A. (2001). *The price of motherhood: Why the most important job in the world is still the least valued.* New York: Henry Holt.

Csikszentmihalyi, M. (1990). *Flow: The psychology of optimal experience.* New York: Harper Perennial.

Danon, P. (2001). *Enlightened values: Is shareholder or stakeholder value the better path?* Unpublished British Telecommunications report.

Deger, S., & Gibson, L. A. (Eds.). (2007). *The book of positive quotations* (2nd ed.). Minneapolis: Fairview Press.

Dirkx, J. (1995). *Earning a living or building a life? Reinterpreting the meaning of work in the practice of workplace education.* Paper presented at the Academy of Human Resource Development Conference, San Antonio, TX.

Dolet, P. (2003). *An exploration of the meaning of work and life: As described by professional midcareer mothers.* Unpublished doctoral dissertation, George Washington University, Washington, DC.

Drucker, P. F. (1974). *Management: Tasks, responsibilities, practices.* New York: Harper & Row.

Dubin, R. (1976). Work in modern society. In R. Dubin (Ed.), *Handbook of work, organizations, and society* (pp. 5–34). Chicago: Rand McNally.

Edmondson Bell, E.L.J., & Nkomo, S. M. (2001). *Our separate ways: Black and white women and the struggle for professional identity.* Boston: Harvard Business School Press.

Ehrenreich, B. (2001). *Nickel and dimed: On (not) getting by in America.* New York: Metropolitan Books.

Emmott, B. (2006, December 23). Economics discovers its feelings: Not quite as dismal as it was. *Economist, 381,* 33–35.

England, G. W., & Whitely, W. T. (1990). Cross-national meaning of working. In A. P. Brief & W. R. Nord (Eds.), *Meanings of occupational work: A collection of essays* (pp. 65–106). Lexington, MA: Lexington Books.

Families and Work Institute. (1997). *National study of the changing workforce: Executive summary.* New York: Author.

Families and Work Institute. (2007). *When work works.* New York: Author.

Families and Work Institute. (2008). *2008 guide to bold new ideas for making work work.* New York: Author.

Fishman, C. (1999, January). Sanity Inc. *Fast Company, 21,* 84–91.

Fishman, C. (2007, July). Message in a bottle. *Fast Company, 117.* Retrieved November 1, 2009, from www.fastcompany.com/magazine/117/features-message-in-a-bottle.html

Fornes, S. L., Rocco, T. S., & Wollard, K. K. (2008). Workplace commitment: A conceptual model developed from integrative review of the research. *Human Resource Development Review, 7,* 339–357.

Fox, A. (2009, September 8). *Gap outlet: Second retailer adopts results-only work environment strategy.* Retrieved September 10, 2009, from http://moss07.shrm.org/hrdisciplines/orgempdev/articles/Pages/GapOutletROWE.aspx

Fox, M. (1994). *The reinvention of work.* New York: HarperCollins.

French, W. L., & Bell, C. H. (1998). *Organization development: Behavioral science interventions for organization improvement* (6th ed.). Upper Saddle River, NJ: Prentice Hall.

Galinsky, E. (1999). *Ask the children: What America's children really think about working parents.* New York: William Morrow.

Gallup publishes long-awaited follow-up to bestselling management book. (2006, November 8). *Gallup Management Journal.* Retrieved March 21,

2009, from http://gmj.gallup.com/content/25390/Gallup-Publishes-LongAwaited-FollowUp-Bestselling-Management-Book.aspx

Gap, Inc. (2004). *Facing challenges, finding opportunities: Social responsibility report.* Retrieved August 15, 2009, from www.gapinc.com/GapInc SubSites/csr/documents/Gap_Inc._Social_Responsibility_Report_2000-2004.pdf

Gardner, H., Csikszentmihalyi, M., & Damon, W. (2001). *Good work: When excellence and ethics meet.* New York: Basic Books.

Gardner, J. (1989). The moral aspects of leadership. *National Association of Secondary School Principals Bulletin.* Thousand Oaks, CA: Sage.

Gayle, S. C. (1997). *Workplace purpose and meaning as perceived by information technology professionals: A phenomenological study.* Unpublished doctoral dissertation, George Washington University, Washington, DC.

George, B., Sims, P., McLean, A., & Mayer, D. (2007). Discovering your authentic leadership. *Harvard Business Review, 85,* 129–138.

Gibbons, J. (2006). *Employee engagement: A review of current research and its implications.* New York: Conference Board.

Gibbons, P. (2007). *Spirituality at work: A pre-theoretical overview.* Retrieved September 8, 2008, from www.paulgibbons.net/publications/downloads/SpiritualityAtWork.pdf

Goodell, E. (Ed.). (1999). *Standards of corporate social responsibility.* San Francisco: Social Venture Network.

Gordon, J. R., & Whelan, K. S. (1998). Successful professional women in midlife: How organizations can more effectively understand and respond to the challenges. *Academy of Management Executive, 12*(1), 8–23.

Greene, L., & Burke, G. C., III. (2007). *Beyond self-actualization.* Retrieved September 22, 2008, from http://ecommons.txstate.edu/cgi/viewcontent.cgi?article=1001&context=sohafacp

Greenhaus, J. H., Collins, K. M., & Shaw, J. D. (2003). The relation between work-family balance and quality of life. *Journal of Vocational Behavior, 63,* 510–531.

Greenleaf, R. (1970). *The servant as leader.* Indianapolis: Robert K. Greenleaf Center.

Handy, C. (2002). What's a business for? *Harvard Business Review, 80*(12), 49–55.

Harter, J., Schmidt, F., & Hayes, T. (2002). Business-unit-level relationship between employee satisfaction, employee engagement, and business outcomes: A meta-analysis. *Journal of Applied Psychology, 87,* 268–279.

Harung, H., Jr. (1999). *Value-based management.* Retrieved December 16, 2008, from http://info.emeraldinsight.com.proxygw.wrlc.org/teaching/insights/value.htm

Hastings, R. (2009, March 4). The "what" and "why" of employee engagement. Retrieved March 11, 2009, from www.shrm.org/hrdisciplines/employeerelations/articles/Pages/WhatandWhy.aspx

Herzberg, F., Mausner, B., & Snyderman, B. B. (1959). *The motivation to work* (2nd ed.). New York: Wiley.

Holbrecke, L., & Springett, N. (2004). *In search of meaning in the workplace.* Unpublished Roffey Park Institute Report, West Sussex, UK.

Horner, M. (n.d.). *Creating our personal best.* Retrieved August 29, 2007, from www.workteams.unt.edu/literature/paper-mhorner.html

Howard, A. (Ed). (1995). *The changing nature of work.* San Francisco: Jossey-Bass.

Hutchings, K., & McGuire, D. (2006, February). *Organization diversity and intergenerational conflict: Human resource solutions for achieving organization generation interaction.* Paper presented at the Academy of Human Resource Development Conference, Columbus, OH.

Imel, S. (2002). *Career development for meaningful life work.* Columbus, OH: Eric Clearinghouse on Adult Career and Vocational Education.

Johnson, J.K.M., & Corday, K. (2009). *Changing definitions of families.* Retrieved March 2, 2009, from http://wfnetwork.bc.edu/topic.php?id=15

Kelly, E., & Moen, P. (2007). Rethinking the clockwork of work: Why schedule control may pay off at work and at home. *Advances in Developing Human Resources, 9,* 487–506.

Kubal, D., & Newman, J. (2008). *A case study: Best Buy.* Retrieved February 24, 2009, from www.workforce.com/section/06/ feature/25/51/84/255187_printer.html

Le Guin, U. (1997). *Lao Tzu, Tao Te Ching: A book about the way and the power of the way.* Boston: Shambhala.

Leonard, B. (2008, September 9). *Employee engagement: Creativity can drive retention.* Retrieved July 13, 2009, from www.shrm.org/hrdisciplines/ staffingmanagement/Articles/Pages/CreativityCanDriveRetention.aspx

Levering, R. (2000). *A great place to work: What makes some employers so good (and most so bad)* (2nd ed.). San Francisco: Great Place to Work Institute.

Lockwood, N. R. (2004). Corporate social responsibility: HR's leadership role. *HR Magazine, 49,* 1–10.

Lockwood, N. R. (2007). Leveraging employee engagement for competitive advantage: HR's strategic role. *HR Magazine, 52,* 1–11.

Loehr, J., & Schwartz, T. (2003). *The power of full engagement: Managing energy, not time, is the key to high performance and personal renewal.* New York: Free Press.

Mainero, L., & Sullivan, S. (2006). *The ABC's of a kaleidoscope career.* Retrieved August 8, 2008, from http://changethis.com/25.02.ABCKal

Maister, D. (2000). *True professionalism.* New York: Free Press.

Maslow, A. H. (1943). A theory of human motivation. *Psychological Review, 50*(4), 370–396.

Maslow, A. H. (1954). *Motivation and personality.* New York: Harper.

Maslow, A. H. (1970). *Motivation and personality* (2nd ed.). New York: Harper & Row.

Maslow, A. H. (1971). *The farther reaches of human nature.* New York: Penguin.

McClelland, D. C. (1965). Achievement motivation can be developed. *Harvard Business Review, 43*(6), 6–24.

McGregor, D. (1960). *The human side of enterprise.* New York: McGraw-Hill.

McKee, A. (2008, August 14). *Work-life balance: It's never too late.* Retrieved September 23, 2009, from www.businessweek.com/magazine/ content/08_34/b4097036735217.htm

Mencia, C. (2008, December 1). Turning point: Laughing in the face of change. *Newsweek*, p. 60.

Merriam, S., Caffarella, R., & Baumgartner, L. (2007). *Learning in adulthood: A comprehensive guide* (3rd ed.). San Francisco: Jossey-Bass.

Miller, C. (2008). *Meaningful work over the life course.* Unpublished doctoral dissertation, Fielding Graduate University, Santa Barbara, CA.

Miller, F. A., & Katz, J. H. (2002). *The inclusion breakthrough: Unleashing the real power of diversity.* San Francisco: Berrett-Koehler.

Mitroff, I., & Denton, E. (1999). A study of spirituality in the workplace. *Sloan Management Review, 40,* 83–92.

Morgan, G. (1996). *Images of organizations* (2nd ed.). Thousand Oaks, CA: Sage.

MOW International Research Team. (1987). *The meaning of working.* London, UK: Academic Press.

Nicoll, D. (1984). Grace beyond the rules: A new paradigm for lives on a human scale. In J. D. Adams (Ed.), *Transforming work: A collection of organizational transformation readings* (pp. 9–25). Alexandria, VA: Miles River Press.

Nirenberg, J. (1995). Why aren't we doing better? *At Work, 4,* 18–20.

Overturf, J. (2005, November 9). *Who's minding the kids? Child care arrangements: Winter 2002.* Washington, DC: U.S. Census Bureau.

Peck, M. S. (1978). *The road less traveled: A new psychology of love, traditional values, and spiritual growth.* New York: Simon & Schuster.

Perman, S. (2006, April 26). Test drive your dream job. *BusinessWeek.* Retrieved October 7, 2008, from www.businessweek.com/smallbiz/ content/apr2006/sb20060412_289938.htm

Peters, T. J., & Waterman, R. H. (1982). *In search of excellence: Lessons from America's best-run companies.* New York: Harper & Row.

Pfeffer, J. (1998). *The human equation: Building profits by putting people first.* Boston: Harvard Business School Press.

Porters, L. W., Steers, R. M., Mowday, R. T., & Boulin, P. V. (1974). Organizational commitment, job satisfaction, and turnover among psychiatric technicians. *Journal of Applied Psychology, 59*, 603–609.

Pozzi, D., & Williams, S. (1997). Success with soul. *At Work, 6*(1), 9.

Project Management Course. (2005). *Self-actualization.* Retrieved September 16, 2008, from www.abraham-maslow.com/m_motivation/Self-Actualization.asp

Pruitt, B., & Rapoport, R. (n.d.). *An essay to accompany looking backwards to go forward: A timeline of the work-family field in the United States since World War II.* Retrieved November 1, 2009, from http://wfnetwork .bc.edu/timelines/other/PRessay.pdf

Putnam, R. (2000). *Bowling alone: The collapse and revival of American community.* New York: Simon & Shuster.

Quinn, R., & Stains, G. (1997). *Quality of employment survey.* Retrieved August 15, 2009, from www.icpsr.umich.edu/icpsrweb/ICPSR/studies/07689

Rath, T., & Clifton, D. (2004). The power of praise and recognition. *Gallup Management Journal.* Retrieved March 21, 2009, from http://gmj.gallup .com/content/12157/Power-Praise-Recognition.aspx

Rechtschaffen, S. (1996). *Timeshifting: Creating more time to enjoy your life.* New York: Doubleday.

Richard, S. (1996). Unleashing the human spirit. *At Work, 5*(3), 11–13.

Richards, R. (1995). *Artful work: Awakening joy, meaning, and commitment in the workplace.* San Francisco: Berrett-Koehler.

Robinson, D., Perryman, S., & Hayday, S. (2004). *The drivers of employee engagement.* Retrieved July 13, 2009, from www.employment-studies .co.uk/summary/summary.php?id=408&style=print

Rogers, C. (1959). A theory of therapy, personality, and interpersonal relationships as developed in the client-centered framework. In S. Koch

(Ed.), *Psychology: A study of science* (pp. 238–257). New York: McGraw-Hill.

Rogers, C. (1961). *On becoming a person.* Boston: Houghton Mifflin.

Russel, C. (1993). *The master trend: How the baby boom generation is remaking America.* New York: Plenum.

Sahadi, J. (2007, June 25). *Flex-time, time off—who's getting these perks.* Retrieved February 24, 2009, from http://money.cnn.com/2007/06/25/pf/work_life_balance/index.htm

Schaefer, C., & Darling, J. (1996). *Spirit matters: Using contemplative disciplines in work and organizational life.* New York: High Tor Alliance for Organization and Community Renewal.

Senge, P. (1990). *The fifth discipline: The art and practice of the learning organization.* New York: Doubleday.

Shaver, K. (2008, March 30). Making it: D.C. woman enters new "stage" of her career. *Washington Post Sunday Magazine.* Retrieved March 20, 2009, from www.washingtonpost.com/wp-dyn/content/article/2008/03/25/AR2008032501900.html

Shipler, D. K. (1996). *The working poor: Invisible in America.* San Francisco: Jossey-Bass.

Shuck, M., & Wollard, K. (2008). Employee engagement: Motivating and retaining tomorrow's workforce. *New Horizons in Adult Education and Human Resource Development, 22*(1), 48–53.

Sievers, B. (1984). Motivation as a surrogate for meaning. *Arbeitspapiere des Frachbereichs.* Bergische Universität, Wuppertal, Germany.

Small, L. L. (2009). *Exploratory case study of how workplace community is manifested in the federal government.* Unpublished doctoral dissertation, George Washington University, Washington, DC.

Society for Human Resource Management. (2008a). *Job satisfaction survey report.* Alexandria, VA: Author.

Society for Human Resource Management. (2008b). *Workplace forecast.* Alexandria, VA: Author.

Solomon, R., & Higgins, K. (2003). *The age of German idealism: Routledge history of philosophy* (Vol. 6). London: Routledge.

Spears, L. (2002). *On character and servant-leadership: Ten characteristics of effective, caring leaders.* Retrieved November 1, 2007, from http://chapters.ewb.ca/pages/president/leadership-articles-and-links/On%20Character%20and%20Servant-Leadership.pdf

Stone, A. G., Russell, R. F., & Patterson, K. A. (2004). Transformational versus servant leadership: A difference in leader focus. *Leadership and Organizational Development Journal, 25*(4), 349–361.

Strenger, C., & Ruttenberg, A. (2008). The existential necessity of mid-life change. *Harvard Business Review, 86*(2), 83–90.

Svendsen, D. S. (1997). *A heuristic study of women's attempts to integrate utilitarian and expressive aspects of self through work.* Unpublished doctoral dissertation, George Washington University, Washington, DC.

Tapia, A. (2008). *The millennials: Why this generation will challenge the workplace like no other.* Retrieved July 21, 2008, from www.hewittassociates.com/Intl/NA/en-US/KnowledgeCenter/ArticlesReports/ArticleDetail.aspx?cid=4959

Terkel, S. (1974). *Working: People talk about what they do all day and how they feel about what they do.* New York: Pantheon Books.

ThinkExist.com. (2008). *"Wilfred Grenfell quotes."* Retrieved October 30, 2008, from http://einstein/quotes/wilfred_grenfell/

Thomas, D. A., & Ely, R. J. (1996). Making differences matter: A new paradigm for managing diversity. *Harvard Business Review, 74*(5), 79–90.

Thomas, K. (2000). *Intrinsic motivation at work: Building energy and commitment.* San Francisco: Berrett-Koehler.

Turner, L. (2005). *Patterns of learning in the lives of people who experience meaningful work.* Unpublished doctoral dissertation, George Washington University, Washington, DC.

Vaill, P. B. (1989). *Managing as a performing art: New ideas for a world of chaotic change.* San Francisco: Jossey-Bass.

Vaill, P. B. (1998). *Spirited leading and learning: Process wisdom for a new age.* San Francisco: Jossey-Bass.

Vance, R. J. (2006). *Employee engagement and commitment: A guide to understanding, measuring and increasing engagement in your organization.* Alexandria, VA: Society for Human Resource Management.

Webber, A. M. (1998a). Are you deciding on purpose: An interview with Richard Leider. *Fast Company, 13,* 114–118.

Webber, A. M. (1998b). Danger: Toxic company. *Fast Company, 19,* 152–161.

Weisbord, M. R. (1987). *Productive workplaces: Organizing and managing for dignity, meaning, and community.* San Francisco: Jossey-Bass.

Welch, J. (2005, April 4). On work and family. *Newsweek.*

Wells, S. (2007). Are you too family friendly? *HR Magazine, 52*(10), 35–39.

WFD Consulting. (2006). *The new career paradigm: Attracting and retaining critical talent.* Newton, MA: American Business Collaboration for Quality Dependent Care.

Wile, S. L. (2001). *Building community in the workplace.* Unpublished doctoral dissertation, Seattle University, WA.

Wilensky, H. (1960). Work, careers, and social integration. *International Social Science Journal, 12,* 543–560.

Wiley, J. W. (1996). Linking survey results to customer satisfaction and business performance. In A. I. Kraut (Ed.), *Organizational surveys: Tools for assessment and change* (pp. 330–359). San Francisco: Jossey-Bass.

Winning Workplaces. (2008). *Top small workplaces 2008.* Retrieved September 7, 2009, from http://online.wsj.com/public/resources/documents/TopSmallWorkplaces08summary.pdf

World Business Council for Sustainable Development. (2000). *Corporate social responsibility: Making good business sense.* Conches-Geneva, Switzerland: Author.

INDEX